S0-AKW-662

FROM THE WORK BY
JONATHAN EDWARDS

Religious Affections

A Christian's Character Before God

EDITED BY
Dr. James M. Houston

INTRODUCTION BY
Charles Colson

BETHANY HOUSE PUBLISHERS
MINNEAPOLIS, MINNESOTA 55438

Religious Affections
Copyright © 1984, 1996
James M. Houston

Cover design by Eric Walljasper

Originially published in 1984 by Multnomah Press.

Scripture references in this volume are a paraphrase by Jonathan Edwards.

All rights reserved. No part of this publication may be reproduced, stored in a retrieval system, or transmitted in any form or by any means— electronic, mechanical, photocopying, recording, or otherwise—without the prior written permission of the publisher and copyright owners.

Published by Bethany House Publishers
A Ministry of Bethany Fellowship International
11400 Hampshire Avenue South
Minneapolis, Minnesota 55438
www.bethanyhouse.com

Printed in the United States of America by
Bethany Press International, Minneapolis, Minnesota 55438

ISBN 1–55661–829–8

DR. JAMES M. HOUSTON was born to missionary parents who served in Spain. From 1949-1971, Dr. Houston was University Lecturer at Oxford University, England. He was a Fellow of Hertford College 1964-1971, and Founding Principal of Regent College, Vancouver, 1968-1978. From 1978 to the present, he has served Regent as Chancellor and Professor of Spiritual Theology.

Dr. Houston has been active in the establishment and encouragement of lay training centers across the continents. These include the C. S. Lewis Institute in Washington, D.C., and the London Institute for the Study of Contemporary Christianity.

He has edited, paraphrased, or translated ten Classics of Faith and Devotion (Multnomah, 1982-1989), and has written *I Believe in the Creator* (Eerdmans, 1980); *The Transforming Friendship* (Lion, 1989); *In Search of Happiness* (Lion, 1990); and *The Heart's Desire* (1992), the last three published again by NavPress in 1996.

CLASSICS OF FAITH AND DEVOTION
Edited by James M. Houston

Mind on Fire by Blaise Pascal
Real Christianity by William Wilberforce
Religious Affections by Jonathan Edwards
Sin and Temptation by John Owens
A Life of Prayer by Clayton L. Berg, Jr.

CONTENTS

Part I: The Nature and Importance of the Affections

THE AFFECTIONS AS EVIDENCE OF TRUE RELIGION
Religious affections are strong and vigorous actions of
the will and heart. They motivate the soul either to
cleave to and seek or to turn away and oppose. Scripture reflects their significance in true religion. Without
holy affections, it is impossible to have true faith.

Part II: How the Religious Affections May Be Falsely Appraised

FALSE SIGNS OF TRUE RELIGIOUS AFFECTIONS
The Pharisees talked much about their religion. Satan,
like the Holy Spirit, is able to bring Scripture to mind;
he is a master counterfeiter. We need to guard against
judging the affections by such false evidences as these.

Part III: The Distinguishing Signs of
Truly Gracious and Holy Affections

HOW TRULY GRACIOUS AFFECTIONS
ARE KNOWN
True spiritual affections are divinely given. Only the
Holy Spirit can make us spiritual by adopting us and
giving us the nature of Christ in His Sonship.

THE OBJECT AND FOUNDATION OF GRACIOUS
AFFECTIONS
The basis of affections is the excellence and nature of
divine things. True affections cannot begin with self-
love. They begin with delighting in the beauty and
holiness of God Himself.

THE FORMATION OF GRACIOUS AFFECTIONS
Gracious affections are developed from a spiritually enlightened mind. This spiritual light reveals the glory of
divine things.

CERTAINTY AND HUMILITY IN GRACIOUS
AFFECTIONS
A true Christian has a conviction of the truth of the
gospel and this conviction causes him to see his sinfulness and his need of God to change him. True humility
comes as he gains a more accurate perspective of who
he is before an infinite and loving God.

GRACIOUS AFFECTIONS CHANGE US TO BE
MORE CHRIST-LIKE
If a person's conversion is real, it will bring about deep
and abiding changes throughout his life. He will be
more holy, gentle, and forgiving. He will become more
and more like Christ.

PREFACE TO THE CLASSICS OF FAITH AND DEVOTION

With the profusion of books now being published, most Christian readers require some guidance for a basic collection of spiritual works that will remain lifelong companions. This new series of Christian classics of devotion is being edited to provide just such a basic library for the home. Those selected may not all be commonly known today, but each has a central concern of relevance for the contemporary Christian.

Another goal for this collection of books is a reawakening. It is a reawakening to the spiritual thoughts and meditations of the forgotten centuries. Many Christians today have no sense of the past. If the Reformation is important to them, they jump from the apostolic Church to the sixteenth century, forgetting some fourteen centuries of the work of the Holy Spirit among many devoted to Christ. These classics will remove that gap and enrich their readers by the faith and devotion of God's saints through all history.

And so we turn to the books, and to their purpose. Some books have changed the lives of their readers. Notice how Athanasius's *Life of Antony* affected Augustine or William Law's *A Serious Call to a Devout and Holy Life* influenced John Wesley. Others, such as Augustine's *Confessions* or Thomas à Kempis's *Imitation of Christ*, have remained perennial sources of inspiration throughout the ages. We sincerely hope those selected in this series will have a like effect on our readers.

Each one of the classics chosen for this series is deeply significant to a contemporary Christian leader. In some cases, the thoughts and reflections of the classic writer are mirrored in the leader's genuine ambitions and desires today, an unusual pairing of hearts and minds across the centuries. And thus these individuals have been asked to write the introduction on the book that has been so meaningful to his or her own life.

EDITING THE CLASSICS

Such classics of spiritual life have had their obstacles. Their original language, the archaic style of later editions, their length, the digressions, the allusions to bygone cultures—all make the use of them discouraging to the modern reader. To reprint them (as was done on a massive scale in the last century and still so today) does not overcome these handicaps of style, length, and language. To seek the kernel and remove the husk, this series involves therefore the abridging, rewriting, and editing of each book. At the same time we sought to keep to the essential message given in the work, and to pursue as much as possible the original style of the author.

The principles of editing are as follows. Keep sentences short. Paragraphs are also shortened. Material is abridged where there are digressions or allusions made that are time-binding. Archaic words are altered. Spelling is that of Webster's Dictionary. Logical linkage may have to be added to abridged material. The identity of theme or argument is kept sharply in mind. Allusions to other authors are given brief explanation. And marginal readings are added to provide concise summaries of each major section.

For the Christian, the Bible is the basic text for spiritual reading. All other devotional reading is secondary and should never be a substitute for it. Therefore, the allusions to Scripture in these classics of devotion are searched out and referenced in the text. This is where other editions of these books may ignore the scriptural quality of these works, which are inspired and guided by the Bible. The biblical focus is always the hallmark of truly Christian spirituality.

Purpose for the Classics: Spiritual Reading

Since our sensate and impatient culture makes spiritual reading strange and difficult for us, the reader should be cautioned to read these books slowly, meditatively, and reflectively. One cannot rush through them like a detective story. In place of novelty, they focus on remembrance, reminding us of values that remain of eternal consequence. We may enjoy many new things, but values are as old as God's creation.

The goal for the reader of these books is not to seek information. Instead, these volumes teach one about living wisely. That takes obedience, submission of will, change of heart, and a tender, docile spirit. When John the Baptist saw Jesus, he reacted, "He must increase, and I must decrease." Likewise, spiritual reading decreases our natural instincts, to allow His love to increase within us.

Nor are these books "how-to" kits or texts. They take us as we are—that is, as persons, and not as functionaries. They guide us to "be" authentic, and not necessarily to help us to promote more professional activities. Such books require us to make time for their slow digestion, space to let their thoughts enter into our hearts, and discipline to let new insights "stick" and become part of our Christian character.

James M. Houston

EDITOR'S NOTE ABOUT JONATHAN EDWARDS AND THE RELEVANCE OF THIS CLASSIC

This work of Jonathan Edwards is of special value today because of the lack among Christians of a spiritual cultivation of the interior life and its affections. I hope that you, as a reader, will not be impatient nor reject Edwards's probing of your heart and affections. Eventually he will help you see how the true Christian life depends upon the cultivation of the right inclinations of the will and of the affections for godly living. Just as the pragmatist has no friends because he simply "uses" people, so pragmatic Christians—and they are indeed numerous today—use God and do not realize the need to know Him intimately. They simply speak in His name and by His authority without allowing their own affections to be nurtured toward Him.

Occasionally we are privileged to meet princes. Jonathan Edwards is acclaimed as both a prince in the world of the thought, as well as in the realm of Christian faith. Like Augustine and Calvin, he stands as one of the greatest leaders of the Church universal.

HIS LIFE

Jonathan Edwards (1703-1758) was the only son of twelve children born into a pioneer family on the frontier of East Windsor, Connecticut. His father, Timothy, was a pastor. Edwards went to

Yale College at the age of thirteen years and graduated in 1720. After two years teaching experience in New York, and some teaching at Yale, he became assistant pastor to his grandfather, Solomon Stoddard. During a ministry of sixty years, his grandfather had built up a fashionable church at Northampton. Edwards became pastor after his grandfather's death and served there for twenty-two years.

Edwards was deeply disturbed by the low spiritual state of his congregation. This changed about 1734 when he began to preach more about justification by grace through faith. He also began to see that true church membership should belong only to those who were truly living this reality in their own lives. Membership and communion were not for those who were merely nominal Christians. A series of conversions began in his church, and then the isolated renewals of scattered congregations were swept into the Great Awakening, which was led by George Whitefield. As the excitement of this religious revival intensified, Edwards attempted in his preaching and writings to advocate a thoughtful and responsible religion of the heart. During this revival, in 1746, Edwards wrote the *Treatise Concerning the Religious Affections*.

But when he began to teach the need for Christians to be truly committed when admitted to the Lord's table, resentment began to build up against him. In 1750 the majority of his congregation voted him out. At the age of forty-six, Edwards found himself dismissed from his pastorate, with seven dependent children, and no prospects of another suitable position. So for the next six years he ministered at a mission outpost consisting of 12 white and 250 Indian families.

In 1757 he was invited to become President of Princeton, but it was too late to enjoy a vindication of his good name. He died a month after arriving at Princeton. Such then is the man whose classic we now introduce.

MISUNDERSTANDINGS OF JONATHAN EDWARDS

Spiritual princes are easily misunderstood. A scholar, metaphysician, and one of North America's greatest thinkers, Edwards has been eulogized by secular intellectuals who have not known his heartbeat. He had a simple, homespun Christian faith. Being a child of God was infinitely more important to Edwards than being a precocious Yale graduate. But the halls of academia don't know how to deal with his devotion to God, except to view it as an eighteenth-century cultural phenomenon that is now antiquated. Similar to John Locke's and Isaac Newton's metaphysics, Edwards's faith is viewed as belonging to a man of his time period. Scholars see his work on *The Freedom of the Will* (1754) only as the genius of abstract reasoning. They never see that his philosophy did not dictate his biblical faith.

Ironically, scholarly admiration tends to bury Edwards. It does not let his voice speak to the conscience of modern man. Yes, he will be remembered for the *faux pas* in once preaching a sermon entitled "Sinners in the Hands of an Angry God" (1741), but even this may be overlooked as only one sermon among over 1200 others that are in manuscript form in Yale Library! Many who would be quite comfortable with Edwards as a deist feel his personal faith and religious affections are too much of an exposure for detached scholarship. All of which goes to show that many who have researched Edwards do not know the man, for they reject his personal faith. They want to know his aesthetic principles but they do not want to know his God.

Edwards has been accused of being unreadable. Even the sympathetic Christian, Alexander Smellie, in the preface to the 1898 edition of the *Religious Affections* speaks of "the indubitable sadness" in the tone of the book, and of the "prevailing atmosphere that is of October rather than of May." It is said that Edwards paid small attention to the graces of diction and as a result his sentences are often long and too complex for the modern reader. But after rewriting his text, I reject this unfair charge. He has a deep perception of truth and its consequences and conveys his message with clarity, exactitude, and pointedness. All I have attempted to do in rewriting his text is to reduce the number of biblical references, to simplify his sentences, and to reduce the wide amplification of his points. In these matters, he may be accused of being too thorough. But then, his world was more leisurely than ours, and he was undistracted by the broken staccato that has been imposed upon our television generation, with its short attention span.

EDWARDS, THE LAST OF THE PURITANS

If Bernard of Clairvaux has been described as the "last of the Fathers," Jonathan Edwards was the last of the great Puritans—at least in New England. All his roots were in the theology of the founding fathers of New England—men such as Thomas Shepard, whom he quotes frequently. Even if he is not so well-versed in the writings of the Puritans as Charles Haddon Spurgeon was to be a century later, he was their theological match with his rejection of Arminianism, and his recognition of the free, omnipotent God upon whom man is utterly dependent. True religion for Edwards was a supernatural gift of God's Holy Spirit, and will be evidenced in responsive affections. Until man has the presence of the Holy Spirit in his life, all his natural, spiritual desires and activities remain carnal in the Pauline sense that is described in Romans.

This Puritan view of Christian piety is based upon the Holy Scriptures alone. As is evidenced in his sermons and other writings, Edwards fed and saturated himself in the Bible throughout his life. In scriptural exegesis he had the acumen of a John Calvin or a John Owen.

Edwards also had the earnestness of a great Puritan preacher. He saw the threefold necessity of helping men understand the gospel theologically, feel passionately its truth, and respond wholly to its reality. George Whitefield, like Billy Graham today, was accused of "enthusiasm" in the 1740 revival of New England. Edwards ran to the defense of such passionate preaching, saying:

> An increase in speculative knowledge in divinity is not what is so much needed by our people as something else. Men may abound in this sort of light, and have no heat. . . . Our people do not so much need to have their heads turned as to have their hearts touched; and they stand in the greatest need of that sort of preaching which has the greatest tendency to do this.

Edwards spoke from powerful convictions, as demonstrated by the thoroughness of his explanations, the fullness of his careful reasoning, and the solemnity of his delivery. The result was his audience could not forget what he said. They came away with an inward fervor that stirred the depths of their heart and shook the foundations of their thoughts.

Edwards esteemed the necessity of having "a rational brain." He demanded that all things in the soul of man should be governed by reason, the highest faculty of our being. "Without the capacity of rational argument, all our proof of God ceases," he argued. Reason can be trusted to reach rationally convincing, theological conclusions. Yet reason, Edwards argued, was insufficient without revelation. He pointed out:

> A person may have a strong reason and yet not have a good reason. He may have a strength of mind to drive an argument, yet not hold even balances. It is not so much from a defect of the reasoning process, as from a fault of the dispositions—if by the dictate of the understanding is meant what reason declares to be best or most for the person's happiness taken in the whole of his duration, it is not true that the will always follows the last dictate of the understanding.

Because of man's depravity, Edwards recognized that reason itself, competent as it may be, is drawn into the complicity of a corrupt human nature. Unaided, human reason cannot be expected to eradicate sin, or to accept its own limitations. Human nature's futility is in self-love infesting our reason, our conscience, and our world. So the mind is also fallen, crippled by sin. Therefore, man needs more than good intentions. He needs the power and the presence of the Holy Spirit to reveal God's Word to his mind and to influence his affections. Tragically, in our generation "the battle for the Bible" overlooks that the biblical revelation has much more to give than inerrant data. It also changes the hearts of men.

EDWARDS AND THE TRUE NATURE OF SPIRITUAL REVIVALS

When Edwards inherited his grandfather's congregation in 1727, he said they were "dry bones," possessing the form of godliness but denying its living power in God. In 1734 he wrote *Faithful Narrative of the Surprising Work of God*, a description of a revival which challenged this powerless orthodoxy. When the Great Awakening unfolded five years later, many counterfeits of true revival began to appear. Consequently, ministers such as Charles Chauncy validly criticized, as a menace to the churches, the shallow emotionalism and divisive self-righteousness of some converts.

Edwards defended the revival in a work entitled *The Distinguishing Marks of a Work of the Spirit of God* (1741). He stated that it possessed five features of genuine revival: Christ is exhorted, the kingdom of evil is attacked, the Scriptures are honored, sound doctrine is promoted, love for God and man is upheld. But in *Thoughts on the Revival in New England* (1742), Edwards was anxious to expose the falsity of a religiosity that was ultimately rooted in self-love and therefore carnal. All these insights helped him to write *Treatise Concerning the Religious Affections*, a masterful treatment of an issue that is still contemporary. Edwards asserts that to communicate truth in a lifeless way is incongruous, a contradiction. We must have a sense of what we are conveying, and convey it in an effective manner. In today's rationalistic culture, we need to be reminded that thinking can never be a substitute for living. That is thinking at its worst. At its best, thinking is a means of living the truth. The intellect is essentially to be viewed instrumentally, and therefore never as an end in itself. This is a truth that Bernard of Clairvaux, Bonaventura, Pascal, and Kierkegaard have all emphasized.

The mind may exercise its discernment in ethics, for example, in choosing the right course for us to follow. But it is the heart that ultimately chooses, either rightly or wrongly. Yet, argues Edwards, the heart never does choose the right, nor make a choice free of self-love. The only way in which the heart can be freed from the self is in the awareness of the love and grace of God. This the Holy Spirit alone can give to a person. True saints of God, then, are those who have "the sense of the heart" as an abiding, new principle in their characters. This is very different from the ephemeral emotions and commotions of revivalism, as well as the easy believism or activism of so much contemporary life. The latter leave no permanent imprint of godliness upon the personality.

This "sense of the heart" brings about a new and unique knowledge of the grace of God within a person. The child of God is like the child who receives a whole new series of relationships through his adoption into another family. His supernatural adoption elicits new habits of devotion because of his firsthand experience of the

Holy Spirit's workings within his soul. It is an experiential knowledge that supplies its own validation.

Thus, Edwards saw that the nature of true religion lay in having "holy" or "gracious affections." He was not the first to stress this. William Fenner, a Puritan a century earlier, wrote *A Treatise of the Affections* (1642), although Edwards probably never knew this particular work. But the Puritan recognition that "out of the heart are the issues of life" is a biblical tradition that emphasizes the vital need to have "a prepared heart." That the heart is sanctified in receiving justification is evidence of the truth of a justified life.

A Summary of the Religious Affections

Today the Christian faith is being seriously distorted by the ways we organize it, institutionalize it, and propagate it. Edwards maintained there is a distinct religious dimension to living which consists largely of the affections. To attempt to reduce or distort the intrinsic reality of this sphere of human life was, and still is today, a serious matter. Moreover, Edwards saw that personal piety was never so private an affair that it could not be publicly scrutinized and judged as either genuine or false in its character.

In the first section of his classic, Edwards uses the text of 1 Peter 1:8 to remind us that persecution is always a good test to reveal what is genuine about the religious life. It helps us to begin to distinguish between "false" and "gracious affections." Edwards also distinguishes between affections and passions. The latter are dark, uncontrollable emotions that obstruct the formation of "gracious affections." Edwards identified love as the master affection, the spring of all other affections. Illustrating conclusively from many Scriptures, Edwards shows how central is the part played by the affections in the thought and language of the Bible.

In the second part Edwards describes those signs which indicate false affections. He is particularly concerned with people who confine the presence and power of the Holy Spirit to a limited sphere of operation. He is also skeptical that mere activity such as reading, praying, singing, or strong self-confidence in one's religious activities is a sign of true affections. Yet we are in no position to judge the motives of others, so we must take heed to ourselves.

In the third and largest part of his book, Edwards gives an

exhaustive account of "twelve signs of gracious affections." The first sign states that the presence and power of the Holy Spirit alone is the source of true affections toward God. The origin of gracious affections, according to the second sign, is in viewing God as God. Love for God springs from His own excellence rather than from our need of Him. So, the third sign states, gracious affections are only developed as we delight in God's holiness. The sight of God is then enough to melt and humble us in His presence. Edwards's fourth sign asserts that gracious affections need spiritual understanding, imparted by the Holy Spirit. Without this they remain cold and inadequate.

However, affections, according to the fifth sign, are supported by real, historical evidences. These challenge the unbeliever and reinforce the believer. The sixth sign states that it is our sense of personal inadequacy and our deep need of God that cause gracious affections to flow and go on flowing. Spiritual pride, then, is the most serious cause of blockage to the outflow of the affections. That is why "evangelical humiliation" is so essential to God's people. The seventh sign points to the change of character that results from conversion. Gracious affections cause us to be more Christ-like. The eighth sign reveals that they produce the meek and gentle spirit of Jesus and the ninth states that a person who possesses the gracious affections will be tenderhearted and without the "hardness of heart" which characterizes the ungodly.

In his tenth sign Edwards asserts that such a life will have balance of temperaments and virtues as well as consistency and permanence of character. The more such characteristics are found in a Christian, the more longing there will be for God in one's life. This is the eleventh sign: God in His holiness will seem to appear less attainable, yet the ardor to be closer to Him and more like Him will grow.

And finally, the twelfth sign states that the reality of Christian experience is seen in the practice of its virtues. Without this, Christianity is reduced to a notional system of thought and is not sustained as a formational reality for authentic living. To confess faith in God is therefore to live a life that is governed by godly emotions, such as the fear and reverence of God, repentant sorrow over sin, joy in God's steadfast love, and love toward one's neighbors.

THE TEXT OF THE AFFECTIONS

It is possible that popular rewordings and abridgments of the original text have had the most impact on many people. The first abridgment of the initial edition of 1746 at Boston was made by William Gordon in the first English edition of 1762. The text was shortened by one-third. Working from the abridgment, John Wesley further rewrote it in 1773—this was published in 1801 after Wesley's death. The original was also translated into Dutch (1779) and Welsh (1883). This abridged edition, some two-thirds of the full text, has been based upon the Worcester edition of 1808, but with reference also to the standard Yale text, edited by John E. Smith in 1959 for Yale University Press. The method of abridgment has been to eliminate some of the biblical quotations written in full, substituting the references instead; condensing some of the illustrative material to one example; reducing some of the more expansive digressions; and generally shortening sentences and paragraphs.

Today the Born-Again Movement, which is America's contemporary revival, is in danger of becoming stillborn due to the lack of the spiritual nurture of the "gracious affections." Charles W. Colson, author of *Born Again* and *Loving God*, is uniquely qualified to write the following introductory essay on the relevance of Edwards's *Religious Affections* for our generation. I am deeply grateful to him for his friendship in doing so.

I also wish to express gratitude to Mrs. Jean Nordland and Mrs. Sharon Turnbull for all their help in typing the material of this book. Miss Liz Heaney of Multnomah Press has devoted all of her editorial skills to the improvement and final production of this work.

James M. Houston

INTRODUCTION

When my dear friend Jim Houston invited me to introduce a book in the "Classics of Faith and Devotion" series, I chose the writings of Jonathan Edwards without hesitation.

I did so, first, because I deeply admire Edwards, a man generally regarded as the greatest theologian of American history, and described by some as the greatest intellect North America has produced. A classic preacher and writer who profoundly influenced the Great Awakening of the eighteenth century, he was also a prophet to the church of his day, critiquing the excesses of that same movement. It is that critique, one of his most brilliant writings, that you will read in the pages to follow—the *Treatise on Religious Affections*.

My second reason for choosing Edwards was that it is more than an isolated message to the Christians of his day—it is a classic statement of eternal truth, penetrating and prophetic. The western church—much of it drifting, enculturated, and infected with cheap grace—desperately needs to hear Edwards's challenge.

EDWARDS, THE MAN

But before doing so, let me suggest we meet the man and look at the life of this remarkable scholar, theologian, pastor, university president, missionary, and great thinker. For Edwards's life demonstrates one of the most basic tenets of his religious belief: True doctrine must be lived, demonstrated not only through intellectual assent, but through actions.

Several misconceptions cloud most people's perceptions of Edwards. For many his reputation is built solely on one sermon, "Sinners in the Hands of an Angry God," and one image, that of the hapless sinner dangling by a flimsy, unraveling thread over the raging fires of hell.

That memorable message conjures up an image of Edwards as a sensational fire-and-brimstone preacher, beating his breast at the pulpit and terrifying his flock into repentance and the Kingdom of God.

"Sinners," like all Edwards's sermons, is biblically based, inexorably logical, sprinkled with images to present the realities of the Scriptures to his audience. It was delivered in Edwards's usual style. He leaned on the lectern, rarely looking up as he read the manuscript in a dull monotone. Yet the effect of his vivid imagery and the cogency of his argument elicited dramatic demonstrations of passionate sorrow and repentance from his hearers. The sermon was not merely an attempt to terrify his congregation, as some have suggested; for Edwards accompanied his portrayal of God's wrath with an equally vivid assurance of God's restraining hand and loving grace.

Another common misconception associates Edwards with Puritan America. By the time he was born in 1703, however, America's settlers were no longer necessarily pilgrims seeking religious freedom; they were adventurers drawn to the colonies in search of material prosperity. As one scholar says of the time, "It had become an implicit principle for most Americans that religion was a private affair—the church's business was to encourage personal piety, not to challenge the ethics of a community informed by the profit motive."

Edwards challenged the materialism of his age, insisting that a man's faith was not a matter of convenient church association or socially acceptable religiosity, but a matter of the heart activated by the will. True Christianity, Edwards argued, is demonstrated by actions—*doing*, not just hearing, the Word.

As scholars concentrate on Edwards's brilliant—and often profoundly difficult—writings, the details of his personal life are sometimes ignored. Beginning his studies of Latin, Hebrew, and

Greek at the age of five, Edwards was a precocious youth of immense intellectual curiosity. His first major piece of writing, an exhaustive study of flying spiders, reveals a penetrating mind and a sophisticated knowledge of natural science; it was written when he was eleven years old.

Edwards entered Yale University at thirteen and graduated at seventeen. He stayed on to continue his master's studies and to teach. In 1726 he was called as an assistant minister at Northampton Church in Northampton, Massachusetts, pastored by his grandfather, Solomon Stoddard. When Stoddard died soon after, Edwards became pastor; in 1727 he married Sarah Pierrepont. Their union, which was to produce twelve children, was a lifelong bond of unusual romance, kindled by their common commitment to Christ and relationship with Him.

Although a frail man plagued by ill health, Edwards spent thirteen hours each day in his office, studying the Scriptures, praying, and counseling his congregation. Particularly after renewal swept his church in 1734, parishioners flocked to Edwards for counsel. Contemporary accounts note that area taverns lost many of their customers; people stopped confiding in their local bartenders and instead turned to Edwards for spiritual insight and practical help.

If Edwards was a stern minister who sadistically enjoyed terrifying his congregation with visions of hell, as some have written, he certainly could not have been such an accessible confidante for his flocks. His heart of warmth and compassion demonstrates otherwise. Upholding Christ as the model, Edwards states: "truly gracious affections . . . are attended with the . . . spirit and temper of Jesus Christ . . . they naturally beget and promote such a spirit of love, meekness, quietness, forgiveness and mercy, as appeared in Christ."

Edwards's sole recreation was daily horseback riding; he loved the quiet woods, which proved fertile ground for thought. Always prepared, he would take a pen and scraps of paper wherever he went. As he rode, he would jot down thoughts, pinning them to his lapels for transfer to a journal upon his return—thus causing comments that Pastor Edwards could go out for a ride at noon on a warm summer's day and return looking like he had come through a snowstorm, covered with tiny scraps of white paper.

A PROPHETIC VOICE

Edwards was at the heart of the Great Awakening of 1740; his own church had experienced a wave of renewal even before revival began to sweep other colonies. Soon, however, he found himself playing the dual role of both defender and critic.

As the Awakening's emotional excesses, demonstrated by enthusiastic converts (swoonings, shrieking, convulsions, and the like), generated criticism from observers, Edwards defended the work of the Spirit in sometimes dramatically convicting sin. But he also acknowledged that whenever a great work of God is at hand, there is a corresponding temptation for the work of the flesh. And in 1742, he delivered a series of sermons warning that Satan had indeed taken a prominent role in affairs. His ruminations led him to realize how urgent it was for Christians to discern the true marks of a person's repentance and new life in Christ.

This was the genesis of his brilliant *Religious Affections*—a work that demonstrates Edwards's commitment to the biblical truth that true faith is manifested by fruits of the repentant sinner's gratefulness to a merciful God.

At mid-century, Edwards's relationship with his church began to sour as he began to dispute a church practice, the Halfway Covenant, established by his grandfather. As the name implies, this edict was a compromise which bent to the political expedience of the day.

Since it was socially advantageous to be associated with a local church, the covenant gave people church membership and the opportunity to baptize their children (though they were excluded from participation in the Lord's Supper and church voting matters), even if they had not proclaimed commitment to Christ or willingness to pursue obedience to His commands.

And in the courageous example of a man standing on his convictions rather than surrendering to social and political pressures, Edwards rejected the Halfway Covenant. In an emotionally charged sequence of events, his congregation turned against him, calling for a vote for his dismissal.

Edwards did not speak in his own defense, but asked that he be judged only by those who had heard him preach or who had read his writings on the subject at hand. This request was denied him and he withdrew from the battle, saying that vindication was not his responsibility, but God's.

The congregation voted 200 to 20 against Edwards; years later, however, the ringleader of that movement came forward—evidently tortured by guilt—and published in a Boston newspaper a lengthy apology for his part in Edwards's dismissal.

After six months of unemployment, Edwards was called to pastor a local church at Stockbridge, Massachusetts, and to serve as a missionary to the Indians. Although the difficulties of life there ravaged his health, his love for the Indians engendered a powerful ministry. During that time several of his major works, including his *Treatise on Freedom of the Will* and *Treatise on Original Sin*, were written. These brought Edwards a theological and intellectual reputation extending throughout North America and abroad.

In 1757 the president of Princeton University, Edwards's son-in-law, Aaron Burr, Sr., suddenly died; the university called Edwards as president. Claiming he was unqualified as a public speaker, he reluctantly took the position.

At that time smallpox was a killer in the colonies. It had also become sermon material for many ministers, some preaching fervently against the experimental vaccines being introduced, others sermonizing in their favor. Edwards didn't pontificate upon the benefits of smallpox research; he simply offered himself as a candidate for vaccination.

Due to his frail condition, he had a severe reaction to the inoculation, then contracted the disease; five weeks after assuming the presidency of Princeton, Jonathan Edwards was dead at age 55.

THE MODERN VOID

Jonathan Edwards's works live today as Christian classics. To fully appreciate their penetrating relevance to Western culture more than two centuries after they were written, we need to take a discerning look at our world today.

It strikes me that the prevalent characteristics of our culture today are rampant narcissism, materialism, and hedonism. Our culture passes itself off as Christian, with fifty million Americans, according to George Gallup, claiming to be "born-again." But it is dominated almost entirely by relativism. The "do your own thing" mindset has "liberated" us from the absolute structure of faith and belief and set us adrift in a sea of nothingness.

We have, to an alarming degree, become victims of our own mindless conformity—self-absorbed, indifferent, empty of heart, the "hollow men" that T. S. Eliot wrote about in the early 1900s. Nihilism predominates in this spiritless age.

A tragic example of this was the death of David Kennedy, third son of Senator Robert Kennedy. A grieving friend said, ". . . in David's case, there was nothing to connect to in life. Even free of the drug influence, there was a deep, overpowering sense of nihilism in his personality. No person, no job, no hobby could give him something to plug into."

That void is what Dorothy Sayers, the astute contemporary of C. S. Lewis, called "the sin that believes in nothing, cares for nothing, seeks to know nothing, interferes with nothing, enjoys nothing, hates nothing, finds purpose in nothing, lives for nothing, and remains alive because there is nothing for which it will die."

That nothingness is an underlying premise for the *Treatise on the Affections*. Edwards stressed that the affections were the "spring of men's actions." Since man is by nature inactive, all activity ceases unless he is moved by some affection. Edwards wrote, "Take away love and hatred, all hope and fear, all anger, zeal, and affectionate desire, and the world would be in a great measure motionless and dead; there would be no such thing as activity amongst mankind, or any earnest pursuit whatsoever."

Though he may have been speaking abstractly about the nature of life in the vacuum of affections, his words closely parallel those of Dorothy Sayers and are tragically insightful for our times.

For in today's stupified, egocentric, materialistic society, it's clear to see that the great conquering tyrant is not totalitarianism; it is nihilism. We, as a culture, have yielded to the insidious enslavement of self-gratification. The villain, in short, is in us.

Too extreme a view? Consider just these few manifestations:

In the name of the "right" of a woman to *control her own body*, 1.5 million unborn children were murdered in America last year. More humans have been disposed of in the United States since the legalization of abortion in the 1970s than during the Holocaust in World War II. Who, I might ask, has inflicted a more widespread tyranny—Hitler, a maniacal dictator, or our uncaring, indifferent society? A few "religious fanatics" may rant and rave, but most people are unmoved by these deaths.

As society we've believed Socrates's assertion that sin is the result of ignorance, and Hegel's, that man is evolving to superior moral levels through increasing knowledge. We've done away with any sense of individual responsibility.

What delusions! In this, the most educated and technically advanced society the world has ever known, we have a divorce rate which until last year had increased steadily for twenty years, soaring crime rates, widespread child abuse, countless shattered families. A valueless culture breeds the most awful tyranny.

As a nation we have been blessed with unprecedented material abundance; but what it has produced is a boredom so pervasive that drug use is epidemic. An extremely successful businessman told me recently that he had discovered a great untapped potential business, drug and alcohol rehabilitation. "It's the fastest growth industry in America, with surefire profits," he said. The recent increase in alcohol and drug addiction has been so dramatic that the size and number of our facilities are inadequate.

Small wonder that the American critic Leslie Fiedler has concluded, "Western man has decided to abolish himself, creating his own boredom out of his own affluence. . . . having educated himself into imbecility and polluted and drugged himself into stupefaction, he keels over, a weary, battered old brontosaurus, and becomes extinct."

The obsessive egocentricity of culture today—narcissism—creates a special tyranny of its own. A *Psychology Today* article cites a young woman, her nerves shot from too many all-night parties, her life an endless round of pot, booze, and sex—who when asked by a therapist, "Why don't you stop?" replied, "You mean I really don't have to do what I want to do?"

Who's the tyrant in a hedonistic society? No totalitarian monster. Something much worse. It's us.

A CRIPPLED CHURCH

But the most frightening fact of our times is that the church of Jesus Christ is in almost as much trouble as our culture.

Unthinkingly, we have almost completely bought into the counterfeit secular value system. Recently I picked up a newspaper and
read on the editorial page the following statement from a prominent Christian leader: "Put God to work for you and maximize
your potential in our divinely-ordered capitalist system."

That is not just bad theology; it is dangerous heresy.

But, sadly, it is typical of much of the Christian message today.
We are saying to the world that we not only accept their value system, but can improve it since God is on our side. And it is this
skewed gospel and cheap grace that prevents the church today
from making any real impact for Christ on our culture.

Christians cannot fight effectively against secularism because
we are riddled with it ourselves. Much of the Christianity we
slickly market is nothing but a religious adaptation of the self-
seeking values of secular culture. The assistant to one renowned
media pastor told me when I asked him the key to this man's suc-
cess: "We give the people what they want." That, too, is heresy.
Heresy is at the very root of the "what's-in-it-for-me" mentality so
prevalent in the west today, a mentality born from the seeds of
materialism planted even in Edwards's day.

The question for the church is not what God can do for us—we
know He loves us—but what are we called to do for Him? How do
we love our God? Loving God calls for more than gushing sen-
timentalities or pious mouthings: Loving God demands obedience
to Him in every aspect of our lives and calling others to obedience—whether that message is popular or not.

EDWARDS'S MESSAGE FOR TODAY

Obedience is at the heart of Edwards's message and he preached
it faithfully, even when it was unpopular. But he discerned the absolute primacy of biblical obedience, particularly to Christ's command that we *be* His witnesses. He would therefore have approved
of A. N. Whitehead's adage that "mathematics is what we do, but
religion is who we are." The quality of personal integrity, living
out the gospel as an individual servant of the living Christ, is a
missing truth in much American religious life today. We've or-
ganized, packaged, sold, politicalized, and institutionalized religion as so many varied products and programs. A person with true

religion is concerned with *who I am before God* and the transformation of personal character wrought by God's grace in the heart.

Edwards relied on the Bible for the proposition that hearing the Word is not enough, nor is the understanding of doctrine. The whole person must be moved by the Holy Spirit to respond in love and gratitude to God. This results in holy living.

With these insights, Edwards struggled against the doctrinaire, rigid theorists of religion on the one hand, and against the unbalanced, emotional enthusiasts on the other. He rejected much of the hysteria, bizarre emotions, and ephemeral enthusiasm associated with the revivalist meetings of his day.

Religious Affections might well have been written for our culture; we've simply substituted the excesses of extreme emotionalism of Edwards's day (though you can switch on some Christian TV channels and see ample demonstrations of that as well) with our more subtle manifestations of cultural Christianity. Many in today's pews use the Christian jargon, participate in all the right prayer breakfasts, small groups, and Christian associations, but their hearts are just as hardened and unrepentant as those to whom Christ will one day say, "Depart—I never knew you."

Edwards stressed that we can never cultivate true religious affection without a deepened sense of sin. It is the very heart of a Christian conversion to confront one's own sin and to desperately desire deliverance from it. And once we've seen our sin, we can only live in gratitude for God's amazing grace.

I know this most intimately. In the throes of Watergate, I went to talk with my friend Tom Phillips. His explanation of having "accepted Christ" baffled me. I was tired, empty, sick of scandal and accusations, but not once did I really see myself as having sinned. Politics was a dirty business and I was good at it. And what I had done, I rationalized, was no different from the usual political maneuverings. What's more, right and wrong were relative, and my motives were for the good of the country—or so I believed.

But that night when I left Tom's house and sat alone in my car, my own sin—not just dirty politics, but the hatred and pride and evil so deep within me—was thrust before my eyes, forcefully and painfully. For the first time in my life, I felt unclean, and worst of all, I could not escape. In those moments of clarity, I found myself driven irresistibly into the arms of the living God. Since that night, I've grown increasingly aware of my own sinful nature; what is good in me I know beyond all doubt comes only through the righteousness of Jesus Christ. Edwards wrote of the same realization twenty years after his conversion:

> I have affecting views of my own sinfulness and vileness, very frequently to such a degree as to hold me in a kind of loud weeping . . . so that I have been often obliged to shut myself up. I have had a vastly greater sense of my own wickedness and the badness of my heart than ever I had before my conversion. . . . It is affecting to think how ignorant I was, when a young Christian, of the bottomless, infinite depths of wickedness, pride, hypocrisy, and deceit left in my heart.

The result of that heightened awareness of sin, Edwards says, is that "the heart will grow in tenderness." And out of that tenderness flows a profound gratitude to God for His mercy, a thankfulness that can only be expressed through service to Him.

Edwards devotes the largest section of his book to this affirmation that: "Gracious and holy affections have their exercise in faith in Christian practice." To have faith in the Word of God must mean to act on it, making a practice of faithful—and radical—holy living. The practice of works of charity toward men—loving our neighbor—is simply acting out the acceptance of the love of God in our heart. A merely notional Christianity is a contradiction that kills vital religion. Edwards saw Christian practice as a sure sign of sincerity. The deed is the most important "outward and visible sign of an inward and spiritual grace." As he said, echoing the Scriptures, "men's deeds are better and more faithful interpreters of their minds than are their words."

But how, we may ask, can practice be used as a test of true Christianity? Edwards does not give an answer. For commitment to Christ is not evidenced through mere conformity to rules, but by having a new heart; what counts is the attitude behind the action. So while we may do Christian things—as crusaders, politicians, or civic-minded citizens—without an authentic, selfless service, our works are empty. It is the Holy Spirit alone who motivates truly, who gives us that vitality that matures into fruitfulness of character, born out of gratefulness to God.

Thus Edwards took a long, hard look at the evidences of true conversion—the fruit that comes from living like Christ. Revivalism is not enough. Political action is not enough. Philanthropy is not enough. Those who promote these modern tendencies of externalizing American religion need to be reinstructed by Edwards's *Affections*. For Edwards concludes:

> There's a kind of external religious practice without any inward experience which is of no account in the sight of God. It is good for nothing. And there is also what is called experience, without any practice, and which is therefore not followed by any Christian behavior. This is worse than nothing. For whenever a person finds within him a heart to relate to God as God, then when he is sent he will always find his disposition is affected in the practical experience of it. If then, religion consists largely of holy affection, it is in the practical exercise of affection which boasts his disposition in true religion . . .

If the reality of the living Christ is to mean anything for twentieth-century Western culture, He must be seen in this way amongst us. The gospel must be revealed through changes in our character, expressed through selfless service in a culture that exalts self. It must be communicated by practical expressions of compassion—sharing the suffering and meeting the needs of the poor, the hungry, the sick, and the imprisoned.

Only through these practical expressions of true religious affections, and of real relationships with the resurrected Christ, can the Christian world view, so battered from within and without, prevail in the twentieth-century void.

Half a century after Edwards, William Wilberforce wrote *Real Christianity*, the first of this series of classics to be republished by Multnomah Press. Wilberforce's example points the way for us.

First, Wilberforce recovered the reality of Christianity in his own personal affections; he lived it out through his tireless crusade for the abolition of slavery. With Europe awash in tidal waves of humanism, he wrote, "Infidelity has lifted up her head without shame," but concluded, "I must confess equally boldly that my own solid hopes for the well-being of my country depend, not so much on her navy and armies, nor on the wisdom of her rulers, nor on the spirit of her people, as on the persuasion that she still contains many who love and obey the Gospel of Christ. I believe their prayers may yet prevail."

There soon followed one of the great revivals of modern times. So, too, is it my belief that the prayers and work of those who love and obey Christ in our world may yet prevail as they keep the message of such a man as Jonathan Edwards. Then, as Edwards envisioned, true Christianity will "be declared and revealed in such a way that instead of hardening spectators, and promoting skepticism and atheism, man will become convinced that there's reality in religion—others seeing their good work, will glorify their Father, which is in heaven."

Charles W. Colson

Part I
THE NATURE AND IMPORTANCE
OF THE AFFECTIONS

I
THE AFFECTIONS AS EVIDENCE
OF TRUE RELIGION

hom having not seen, you love; in whom, though now you see Him not, yet believing, you rejoice with joy unspeakable and full of glory (1 Peter 1:8).

In these words the Apostle describes the state of the minds of those Christians he was writing to who were under persecution. These persecutions are what he is considering in the two preceding verses when he speaks of "the trial of their faith" and of "their being in heaviness through manifold temptations."

Such trials have a threefold benefit for true religion. First, they show what is true religion. For trials tend to distinguish between what is true and what is false. Trials suggest that the authenticity of faith is tested just as gold is tried in the fire. The faith of true Christians which is tried and proven to be true is "found to praise and honor and glory," as the previous verse indicates.

Persecution tests the reality of faith.

These trials, then, are a further benefit to true religion because they not only manifest its truth but they also enhance its genuine beauty and attractiveness. True virtue is loveliest when it is oppressed. The divine excellency of real Christianity is best exhibited when it is under the greatest trials. Then it is "found to praise and honor and glory."

Persecution enhances faith.

3

**Persecution
purifies faith.**

A third benefit of such trials for true religion is that they purify and increase it. They not only show it to be true, they also free it from false admixtures. Nothing is left but that which is real. Trials enhance the attractiveness of true religion. These then are the benefits of persecutions upon true religion that the Apostle is thinking about, in the verse preceding this text.

In the text itself, the Apostle observes how true religion operated in the Christians to whom he wrote and how those benefits of persecution appeared to them. He feels their sufferings reveal two exercises of true religion.

1. Love to Christ

**Love to Christ is
a hidden love.**

"Whom having not seen, you love." The world was ready to wonder what strange principle influenced these Christians to expose themselves to such great sufferings, and to renounce all that was dear and pleasant as the objects of sense. To the world around them they seemed mad, and acted as though they hated themselves because the world could not see anything to induce them to suffer like this or to support them under the carrying of such trials. They had a supernatural love for something that was unseen. They loved Jesus Christ whom they saw spiritually. But the world did not see Him.

2. Joy in Christ

Although their outward sufferings were intensely grievous, these Christians had inward spiritual joys which were greater than their sufferings. These supported them and enabled them to suffer with cheerfulness.

**Joy in Christ is
likewise hidden.**

The Apostle notices two things in this text about joy. First, he notes the manner in which joy arises. Christ, by faith, is the foundation of all joy. This is the evidence of things not seen, "In whom, though now you see Him not, yet believing, rejoice." Second, he notes the nature of this joy. It is "unspeakable and full of glory." It is unspeakable because it is very different from the worldly joys and carnal delights. Its nature is purer and more sublime and heavenly because it is supernatural, truly divine, and so ineffably excellent. No words can describe the sublimity and exquisite sweetness of joy in Christ. It is also unspeakable because God liberally gives Christians this holy joy, and in large measure when they are under the duress of persecution.

Their joy was full of glory. This can be said about it. No words are more suitable to represent its excellence than these. While rejoicing with this joy, their minds were filled with a glorious brightness, and their natures became exalted and perfected. It was a most worthy and noble rejoicing because it did not corrupt and defile the mind as carnal things do. Instead it gave the mind beauty and dignity. The anticipation of the joy of heaven raised their minds to heavenly bliss, and filled them with the light of God's glory, making them shine with the expression of that glory.

Yet this joy is ineffable.

With this meditation in mind I propose the following statement: "True religion, in large part, consists of holy affections."

The Apostle, in observing and commenting upon the effects trials had upon true religion, singles out *love* and *joy* as the two religious affections that were exercised. These affections demonstrate that their religion is both true and pure in its distinct glory. I want first to show what is meant by the affections, and second to notice the ways in which a great part of true religion lies in the affections.

WHAT IS MEANT BY THE AFFECTIONS?

My answer to this question is the affections are the more vigorous and practical exercises of the inclination and will of the soul.

God has endowed the soul with two faculties. One is capable of perception and speculation so that it can

The soul has two faculties.

discern, see, and judge things. This is called the *under-standing*. The other faculty is that by which the soul does not merely perceive and view things, but is in some way inclined toward the things it views or considers. It is either inclined to them or is disinclined and averse from them. The soul, because of this faculty, does not want to see things as an indifferent, unaffected spectator. It either likes or dislikes, is pleased or is displeased, approves or rejects. This faculty is called *inclination*. When it determines and governs actions, inclination is called the will. When the mind is related to these actions, inclination is often called the heart.

Inclination is exercised in two forms. The soul either views things with approval, with pleasure, and with acceptance, or it views things with opposition, with disapproval, with displeasure, and with rejection.

The heart as the affections

These exercises of the inclination and will of the soul have various intensities. Some are almost completely indifferent. But there are other degrees where approbation or dislike, pleasure or aversion are stronger. When the soul reacts vigorously and strongly, the exercise is still more intense. Indeed, because the Creator has bonded body and soul together, even the physical life can be affected by such emotions. Through all cultures and times this faculty has been called the heart. These are those vigorous and sensible exercises of the faculty that we call the *affections*.

So the will and affections of the soul are not two distinct faculties. The affections are not essentially distinct from the will. They differ only in the liveliness and sensitivity of their exercise, not in their expression.

Affections depend upon the intensity of will.

Language is sometimes inadequate since the meaning of words tends to be loose and vague and not defined precisely by customary usage. In one sense the affections of the soul are not different from the will and inclination. But in other ways, the action of will and inclination may not be called *affections*. For in everything we do when we act voluntarily, there is an exercise of the will and inclination. Our inclination governs our actions. But all the actions of inclination and will are not usually called affections. The difference between what is called affections and what is not lies only in the intensity and manner of their exercise. In every act of the will, the will either likes or dislikes, is either inclined or disinclined to what is before it. These are not essentially different from the affections of love and hate. Indeed, the liking or inclination of the soul to something, if it is intense and vigorous, is the very thing which we call the *affection of love*, and the same degree of dislike and disinclination is what we mean by *hatred*. So it is the degree to which the will is active, either toward or against something, that makes it an affection.

Our nature, in the intrinsic unity of the body and soul, is such that a vigorous and intense inclination of the will affects our bodies, too. These laws of the union of the body and soul and its constitution may promote the exercise of the affections. But the mind, not the body, is the proper seat of the affections. The body of a man is not directly capable of thinking and understanding. Only the soul has ideas, and so only the soul is pleased or displeased with its ideas. Since only the soul thinks, only the soul loves or hates, rejoices or is grieved at what it thinks. The bodily effects of these emotions are not the same thing as the affections, and are in no way essential to them. Therefore a disembodied spirit is capable of love and hatred, joy or sorrow, hope or fear, or other affections.

The mind is the seat of the affections.

Although affections and passions are frequently spoken of as the same thing, they are different. *Affection* is a word used with more extensive significance than *passion* and it is used in reference to strong actions of the will or inclination. *Passion* is used of sudden actions and its effects on the body are more violent. The mind is more overpowered and less in control.

Like the exercises of the inclination and will, the affections will either motivate the soul to seek and cleave to what is in view, or turn away the soul and oppose what is in view.

Affections and passions are not the same.

Love, desire, hope, joy, gratitude, and contentment motivate the soul, and hatred, fear, anger, and grief turn it away. Some affections are a mixture of the two responses. For example, the affection of pity motivates the soul toward the person suffering as well as turns it away from the suffering. Zeal contains both a high appreciation of some personal thing and a vigorous antagonism toward what opposes the thing valued. Other mixed affections might be mentioned but I hasten to the next heading.

TRUE RELIGION CONSISTS LARGELY OF THE AFFECTIONS

We may make ten observations to show that true religion consists largely of the affections.

1. True Religion Consists Largely in Strong Inclinations and Will.

The fervent exercises of the heart and lively actions of the inclination and will determine much of true religion. The religion which God requires and will accept does not consist of weak, dull, and lifeless wishes which scarcely raise us above indifference. In His Word, God insists that we be "fervent in spirit" and actively engage our hearts in religion. "Be fervent in spirit, serving the Lord" (Romans 12:11). "And now, Israel, what does the Lord your God require of you but to fear the Lord your God, to walk in all His ways, and to love Him and to serve the Lord your God with all your heart, and with all your soul?" (Deuteronomy 10:12, cf. 6:4, 6; 30:6).

True religion is fervent and serious. We are nothing if we are not in earnest about our faith, and if our wills and inclinations are not intensely exercised. The religious life contains things too great for us to be lukewarm. True religion is always a dynamic thing. Its power is in the inward exercises of the heart. So true religion is called "the power of godliness," to distinguish it from those mere external appearances of religion that are just "the form of godliness." "Having a form of godliness, but denying the power of it" (2 Timothy 3:5). The Spirit of God is a spirit of powerful holy affection in those who have a sound and solid faith. God is said to have "given the spirit of power, and of love, and of a sound mind" (2 Timothy 1:7). Likewise when a person receives the Spirit of God in His saving and sanctifying influences, he is said to be "baptized with the Holy Ghost and with fire." The Spirit of God excites such power and fervor in hearts that they "burn within them," as it was described of the disciples in Luke 24:32.

Faith can be compared to vigorous exercises such as running, wrestling, or straining for a great prize or crown. It can also be used to describe fighting strong enemies who seek our lives as in warfare or the siege of a city or kingdom.

True grace has various degrees. Some are only babes in Christ, and in their inclinations and will toward divine things are still comparatively weak. Others, however, have vigorously exercised the power of godliness, and this enables them to prevail above all carnal or natural affections, and to overcome them effectively. Every true disciple of Christ "loves Him above father and mother, wife and children, brothers and sisters, houses and land; yes, even more than his own life." True religion intensely exercises the will.

2. Affections Are the Mainspring of Human Actions.

The Author of human nature not only gave affections to man but He made them the basis of human actions.

Man's nature is very lazy, unless he is influenced by some affection such as love, hate, desire, hope, or fear. These emotions are like springs that set us moving in all the affairs of life and its pursuits. This is seen in the world of business when affairs are earnestly dealt with and pursued with vigor. The marketplace is seen as the sphere of business and action. If all love and hatred, hope and fear, anger, zeal, and affectionate desire were taken away, the

Affections are the mainspring of human life.

world would be motionless and dead.

Affection, indeed, is the motivation of the covetous man, the man who is greedy in worldly pursuits. The affections push the ambitious man forward in his pursuit of worldly fame. They activate the lustful man in his pursuit of pleasure and sensual delights. The world continues in constant commotion and activity in the pursuit of these things, but if affection were taken away, the source of this activity would be gone and the motion itself would cease. And if this is true of worldly affairs, it is also true in matters of faith. The spring of their actions lies very much in religious affections. He who has only doctrinal knowledge and theory, without affection, is never engaged in the goodness of faith.

3. Religious Matters Only Grip Us to the Degree That They Affect Us.

Notions of God are not enough.   Multitudes often hear the Word of God and have knowledge about it. But it will be totally ineffective and will make no change in their behavior or character if they are not affected by what they hear. Many hear of the glorious affections of God, His almighty power and boundless wisdom, His infinite majesty and His holiness. They are hearers of God's infinite goodness and mercy, His great wisdom, power, and greatness. And in particular they hear of the unspeakable love in Christ and of the great things Christ has done and suffered on their behalf. They also hear the clear commands of God and of His gracious warnings and sweet invitations of the gospel. They hear all this and yet there is no change of heart or of behavior. This is simply because they have not been affected by what they heard.

I am bold to assert that no change of religious nature will ever take place unless the affections are moved. Without this, no natural man will earnestly seek for his salvation. Without this, there is no wrestling with God in prayer for mercy. No one is humbled and brought to the feet of God unless he has seen for himself his own unworthiness. No one will ever be induced to fly in refuge to

Christ as long as his heart remains unaffected. Likewise, no saint has been weaned out of the cold and lifeless state of mind, or recovered from backsliding, without having his heart affected. In summary, nothing significant ever changed the life of anyone when the heart was not deeply affected.

4. The Holy Scriptures Emphasize the Affections.

Everywhere the Scriptures place much emphasis upon the affections: fear, hope, love, hatred, desire, joy, sorrow, gratitude, compassion, and zeal.

The Bible speaks much about the need of godly fear. It is often described as a character of those that are truly devout since they tremble at God's Word and fear Him. His glory and His judgment make them fear. The saints in Scripture are described as "hearers of God" or "they that fear the Lord." Since the fear of God is, to a large extent, the nature of true godliness, it is very commonly described as "the fear of the Lord." Everyone who knows the Bible knows this.

The fear of the Lord is the basis of godliness.

Similarly, hope in God and in the promises of His Word is often spoken of in Scripture as a significant part of true faith. Hope is mentioned as one of the three great things of which religion consists (see 1 Corinthians 13:13). "Hope in the Lord" is also mentioned as the response of the saints. "Happy is he who has the God of Jacob for his help, whose hope is in the Lord his God" (Psalm 146:5). "Blessed is the man that trusts in the Lord and whose hope the Lord is" (Jeremiah 17:7). "Be of good courage, and he shall strengthen your heart, all you that hope in the Lord" (Psalm 31:24). And we might cite many other passages. Fear and hope are joined as constituting the character of true saints: "Behold, the eye of the Lord is upon those that fear Him, upon them that hope in His mercy" (Psalm 33:18). "The Lord takes pleasure in them that fear Him, in those that hope in His mercy" (Psalm 147:11). Hope is viewed as so vital that the Apostle said,

Hope in the Lord is also essential.

12   The Nature and Importance of the Affections

"We are saved by hope" (Romans 8:24). (It is also described as "the helmet" of the Christian soldier [1 Thessalonians 5:8].) Hope is that which remains sure, like the anchor of the soul (Hebrews 6:19). It is also described as a great fruit and benefit received by true saints because of Christ's resurrection (1 Peter 1:3).

The Scriptures place much emphasis on the affection of love to God, to the Lord Jesus Christ, to God's people, and to all mankind. But we shall say more of this later on.

To love God we must hate sin. The opposite affection of love, hatred, has sin as its object. This too is a significant part of true religion in the Scriptures. "The fear of the Lord is to hate evil" (Proverbs 8:13). The saints are called upon to give evidence of their sincerity by doing this. "You that love the Lord hate evil" (Psalm 97:10). The Psalmist often mentions this as evidence of his sincerity. "I will walk within my house with a perfect heart. I will set no wicked thing before my eyes; I hate the work of them that turn aside" (Psalm 101: 2, 3). "I hate every false way" (Psalm 119:104, cf. v. 127). Again in Psalm 139:21: "Do I not hate them, O Lord, that hate You?"

Hunger and thirst after God is true righteousness. Holy desire, which is expressed in longings and hunger and thirst after God, is often mentioned in Scripture as an important part of true religion. "The desire of our soul is to Your name, and to the remembrance of You" (Isaiah 26:8). "One thing have I desired of the Lord and that will I seek after, that I may dwell in the house of the Lord all the days of my life, to behold the beauty of the Lord and to inquire in His temple" (Psalm 27:4). There are many psalms that express similar thoughts: Psalm 42:1, 2; 63:1, 2; 73:25; 84:1, 2; 119:20; 130:6; 143:6, 7; and Song of Solomon 3:1, 2.

Such holy desires and thirst of the soul, according to the Beatitudes, make a man truly blessed. "Blessed are they that do hunger and thirst after righteousness; for they shall be filled" (Matthew 5:6). Participation in this holy thirst is viewed as one of the great blessings of eternal life (Revelation 21:6).

The Scriptures also speak of holy joy as a significant part of true religion. We are often exhorted to exercise this joy. "Delight yourself in the Lord and He will give you the desires of your heart" (Psalm 37:4; cf. Psalm 97:12; 33:1). "Rejoice and be exceeding glad" (Matthew 5:12). Finally, "Brethren rejoice in the Lord" (Philippians 3:1; cf. 4:4). Joy also appears among the fruit of the Spirit (Galatians 5:22). The Psalmist mentions his holy joy as evidence of his sincerity.

Religious sorrow, mourning, and brokenness of heart are often mentioned in reference to true religion. These are frequently described as those qualities which distinguish true saints and are a significant part of their character: "Blessed are they that mourn, for they shall be comforted" (Matthew 5:4). "The Lord is near to them that are of a broken heart, and saves such as be of a contrite spirit" (Psalm 34:18). Thus godly sorrow and brokenness of heart is often referred to as one of the great distinguishing traits of saints that is peculiarly pleasing and acceptable to God. "The sacrifices of God are a broken spirit: a broken and contrite heart, O God, You will not despise" (Psalm 51:17; cf. Isaiah 57:15; 66:2).

Gratitude is another affection mentioned, especially gratitude that is related to thankfulness and praise to God. This is frequently referred to in the Psalms and in many other parts of the Scriptures, so I need not mention particular texts.

The Scriptures often speak of compassion or mercy as a vital feature of true religion. Indeed, a merciful man and a good man are equivalent terms in the Bible: "The righteous shows mercy and gives" (Psalm 37:21). "He that honors the Lord has mercy on the poor" (Proverbs 14:31). "Put on as the elect of God, holy and loved, bowels of mercy" (Colossians 3:12). Those who are truly blessed have this great trait. Our Savior said, "Blessed are the merciful, for they shall obtain mercy" (Matthew 5:7). The

Holy joy

Godly sorrow

Gratitude

Mercy is true sacrifice.

Pharisees failed to show it (Matthew 23:23). The prophet Micah emphasized its importance: "He has shown, O man, what is good; and what does the LORD require of you, but to do justice, and love mercy, and walk humbly with your God?" (Micah 6:8). Hosea 6:6 says, "For I desired mercy and not sacrifice." This text must have excited our Savior, since He recited it twice: once in Matthew 9:13 and again in 12:7.

Zeal for God   Zeal is also spoken of as an essential part of the religion of true saints. It is the great thing Christ had in view in giving Himself for our redemption (Titus 2:14). The lukewarm Laodiceans were rebuked for their lack of zeal (Revelation 3:15, 16, 19).

I have cited a few texts out of the vast number which emphasize that our religion depends much upon the affections. Those who deny this may as well throw away their Bibles and get some other rule by which to judge the nature of religion.

5. Love Is the Chief of the Affections.

Love is the fountain and chief of all other affections. Our blessed Savior illustrates this in His answer to the lawyer's question, "What is the great commandment of the law?" (Matthew 22:37-40). The Apostle Paul also indicates this from time to time: "He that loves another has fulfilled the law" (Romans 13:8). Verse 10 says, "Love is the fulfilling of the law." Also in Galatians 5:14, "For all the law is fulfilled in one word, even in this, you shall love your neighbor as yourself." Moreover we read in 1 Timothy 1:5: "Now the end of the commandment is charity, out of a pure heart." The same apostle speaks of love as the greatest thing in religion and as the heart of it. Without love the greatest knowledge and gifts, the most brilliant profession, in fact everything else which is part of religious life, are vain and worthless. As 1 Corinthians 13 demonstrates, it represents the fountain from which all that is good proceeds.

Such love includes the whole sincere desire of the soul toward God and man. Yet when this inclination of the soul is deliberate in its attempt toward God, it becomes affection or "affectionate love." This is the dynamic and fervent love which Christ describes as the sum of all religion when He speaks of loving God with all our hearts, with all our souls, with all our minds, and our neighbor as ourselves. This love is the sum of all that was thought and prescribed in the law of the prophets.

However, this does not mean that as a summary of all religion this and other Scriptures are excluding the habit or exercise of the mind. But it is true and clear from these Scriptures that the essence of all true religion lies in holy love. It is this divine affection and the habitual disposition toward it which is the foundation and the fruits of all that constitutes true faith.

It is thus clear that a great part of true religion consists in the affections. Love is not just one of the affections; it is the first and chief affection, the strength of the others. From love arises hatred of those things which are contrary to what we want to love or which oppose and frustrate us in those things in which we delight. It is from such exercises of love and hate, depending on the context of these affections either present or absent, certain or uncertain, probable or improbable, that arise all other affections of desire, hope, fear, joy, grief, gratitude, anger, etc. All other religious emotions will arise from such a dynamic, affectionate, and fervent love toward God. From it will come intense hatred or abhorrence of sin, a fear of it, and a dread of God's displeasure. From it also will come gratitude to God for His goodness, serenity, and joy in God for His gracious presence, grief for His absence, a joyful hope when He is anticipated, and a fervent zeal for the glory of God. Similarly, from a fervent love of men will arise all other virtuous affections toward mankind.

Love summarizes all one's being before God.

Love is chief of the affections.

6. Holy Affections Characterize the Saints of the Bible.

Let me cite three eminent saints who have expressed the reality of such affections within their hearts.

David

First is David: "A man after God's own heart." The Psalms present us with a living portrait of his faith. In his holy songs, David left us the expressions and cultivation of devout and holy affections. They communicate his humble and fervent love of God, his admiration for God's glorious perfections and wonderful works, the earnest desires, thirst, and panting of his soul after God, his delight and joy in God, his sweet and melting gratitude toward God for His great goodness, and a holy celebration and triumph of soul in the favor, sufficiency, and faithfulness of God. The Psalms also express David's love toward, and delight in, the saints, who are the excellent of the earth, as well as his great delight in the Word and ordinance of God. He grieves for his own and others' sins, and communicates his fervent zeal for God, as well as his hatred of the enemies of God and His people. The Psalms of David are full of expressions of holy affection. David, in the book of Psalms, does not speak only as an individual. As the Psalmist of Israel, he is also expressive of the foreshadowing of the church of God and of Christ, the leader of the church's praises and worship. Thus many of the psalms speak in the name of Christ personified. In many other psalms David speaks in the name of the Church.

Paul

A second example is the Apostle Paul. Above all others he was a chosen vessel to bear Christ's name to the Gentiles. He was the chief instrument for proclaiming and establishing the Christian church in the world, and for distinctly revealing the glorious mysteries of the gospel for the instruction of the church in all ages. So it is not improper, as some may think, to consider him the most eminent servant of Christ that ever lived. Yet he was a person full of affection. Obviously, the faith he expresses in his epistle consists very much in holy affections. In all his expressions about himself, he was inflamed, motivated, and entirely absorbed in an ardent love for his glorious Lord. He esteemed all things as loss for the excellency of the knowledge of Him. Indeed, he esteemed them but rubbish in order to win Him. He represents himself as being overwhelmed by holy affection. This compelled him to go forward in service in spite of all the difficulties and sufferings (2 Corinthians 5:14, 15).

Paul's epistles are full of expressions of an overwhelming affection toward the people of Christ. He speaks of his dear love for them (2 Corinthians 12:19; Philippians 4:1; 2 Timothy 1:2), his abundant love (2 Corinthians 2:4), and his affectionate and tender love (1 Thessalonians 2:7, 8). He also speaks of his bowels of love (Philippians 1:8; Philemon 12, 20), his earnest care for others (2 Corinthians 8:16), and his bowels of pity or mercy toward them (Philippians 2:1). He expresses his concern for others as anguish of heart (2 Corinthians 2:4). He mentions the great conflict of his soul for them (Colossians 2:1). He speaks of a great and continual grief he had in his heart from compassion for the Jews (Romans 9:2). He speaks of his mouth being open and his heart enlarged toward Corinthian Christians (2 Corinthians 6:11). Often he speaks of his "affectionate and longing desire" (1 Thessalonians 2:8; Romans 1:11; Philippians 1:8; 4:1; 2 Timothy 1:4).

The same apostle expresses the affection of *joy* (2 Corinthians 1:12; 7:7, 9, 16; Philippians 1:4; 2:1, 2; 3:3; Colossians 1:24; 1 Thessalonians 3:9). He speaks of his rejoicing with great joy (Philippians 4:10; Philemon 7), his joying and rejoicing (Philippians 2:1, 2), his rejoicing exceedingly (2 Corinthians 7:13), and of his being filled with comfort and being exceedingly joyful (2 Corinthians 7:4). He speaks of himself as always rejoicing (2 Corinthians 6:10), of the triumphs of his soul (2 Corinthians 2:14) and of his glorying in tribulation (2 Thessalonians 1:4; Romans 5:3).

The affection of *hope* is expressed in Philippians 1:20; he speaks of his "earnest expectation and his hope."

He likewise expresses an affection of godly jealousy (2 Corinthians 11:2, 3). Throughout the Apostle's history after his conversion, he exhibits much *zeal* for the cause of his Master and the interest and prosperity of His church. As a result he was strongly involved in constant and mighty labors in order to instruct, exhort, warn, and reprove others, "travailing in birth with them." He was in conflict with powerful and innumerable enemies who continually opposed him. He describes wrestling with principalities and powers and of not fighting as one who beats the air. He speaks of running the race set before him, continually pressing forward through all kinds of difficulties and sufferings. Others thought him quite mad. Yet the extent of his affection is further demonstrated by his being so full of tears. In 2 Corinthians 2:4 and Acts 20:19 he speaks of his "many tears." In verse 31 he says that he shed tears continually night and day.

If anyone examines the records given in Scripture of this great Apostle but does not see that his religion consisted much in affection, he is willfully blind. He is like one who shuts his eyes so he cannot see the light that is shining in his face.

John   I should also mention the Apostle John as an example. As the beloved disciple who was the nearest and dearest to his Master of any of the twelve, he was admitted to the greatest privileges. He was one of the three who were present with Him on the mount at His transfiguration; and he was at the raising of Jairus's daughter; and Jesus took him with Him when He agonized in the garden. He is also one spoken of by the Apostle Paul as one of the three main pillars of the Church. But above all, he was favored as the one who leaned on his Master's bosom at His Last Supper. He was chosen by Christ to be a disciple to whom He would reveal His dispensations toward His church at the end of time. We have these accounts in the book of Revelation. He is the one chosen to conclude the canon of the New Testament and of the whole of the Scriptures.

It is evident from his writings as has been generally observed by scholars that John was a person remarkably full of affection. His addresses are expressed most tenderly and sympathetically. They breathe nothing but the most fervent love. It is as though he were made up entirely of tender and holy affection. We cannot help seeing that affection filling all his writings.

7. The Lord Jesus Christ Had a Remarkably Tender and Affectionate Heart.

Jesus Christ had a remarkably tender and affectionate heart. He is the shepherd whom the flock should follow. His virtue is expressed much in the exercise of holy affections. His is the most wonderful example of ardor, vigor, and strength of love, both to God and man, that ever was. These affections gave Him the victory in the mighty struggle and conflict of His agonies when "He prayed more earnestly, and offered strong crying and tears" and wrestled in tears and in blood. The power of the exercises of His holy love was stronger than death. In His great struggle He overcame the natural affections of fear and grief, even when He was so amazed and His soul was exceedingly sorrowful even unto death.

During the course of His life, He also appeared to be full of affection. Fulfilling Psalm 69, He had great zeal: "The zeal of your house has eaten me up" (John 2:17). He felt grief for man's sins. "He looked round about on them with anger, being grieved for the hardness of their hearts" (Mark 3:5). He cried when he thought of the sin and misery of ungodly man. When he was viewing the city of Jerusalem and all its inhabitants, He cried: "O Jerusalem, Jerusalem, which kills the prophets and stones them that are sent to you; how often would I have gathered your children together, as a hen gathers her brood under her wings, and you would not!"

We also read of Christ's earnest desire: "With desire have I desired to eat this passover with you before I suffer" (Luke 22:15). We often read of the affection of piety or compassion in Christ (Matthew 15:32; 18:27; Luke 7:13) and of His being moved with compassion (Matthew 9:36; 14:14; Mark 6:34). How tender He was when, mourning their brother, Mary and Martha came to Him with their complaints and tears (see John 11)! And how wonderfully affectionate was His last and dying discourse with His eleven disciples the evening before He was crucified. He told them He was going away and foretold the great difficulties and sufferings they would meet with in the world when He was gone; He comforted and counseled them as His dear little children. He bequeathed to them His Holy Spirit and in so doing He gave them His peace and His comfort and joy as His last will and testament (see John 13-16). He concluded with an affectionate intercessory prayer for them and for His whole Church in chapter 17. Of all the discourses ever penned or uttered, this seems to be the most affectionate and affecting.

8. The Religion of Heaven Consists Largely of Affection.

Doubtless there is true religion in heaven, and true religion in its utmost purity and perfection. According to the Scripture, the representation of that heavenly state consists largely in holy and mighty love and joy. The expression of these is given in the most fervent and exalted praises. So the religion of the saints in heaven consists of the same things as the religion of the saints on earth, namely love and joy unspeakable and full of glory.

The earthly love and joy of the saint is a taste of heaven.

It is true that we do not know experientially what it means to have love and joy in the world out of the body, or indeed in a glorified body. We have not had this kind of experience. But the saints on earth do know what divine love and joy in the soul can be. We also know that our love and joy are of the same kind as those which are experienced in heaven. For the love and joy of the saints on earth are only the beginning and the dawning of that light, life, and blessedness of heaven. It is only the degree and the circumstances that are different now. This is evident from many Scriptures such as Proverbs 4:18; John 4:14; 6:40, 47, 50, 51, 54, 58; 1 John 3:15; 1 Corinthians 13:8-12. It is unreasonable, therefore, to suppose that the love and the joy of the saints in heaven, although not of the same degree and circumstances as love and joy on earth, are so different that they are not affections. This we do not believe.

Therefore the religion of heaven also consists chiefly in holy love and joy, and so very much in affection. The way to learn the true nature of anything is to go to where that thing is found in purity and affection. So if we wanted to see the true nature of gold we would look at it not in the natural state of ore, but after it had been refined. And with true religion we look and see it in its highest perfection, not when it is with defect or mixture. All who are truly devout are not of this world, for they are strangers here and belong to heaven. They are born from above and heaven is their native country. So the principle of true religion which is in them is the imparting of the religion of heaven. Their grace is the glory of God. God fits them for that world by conforming them to it.

9. God's Ordinances and Duties Are the Means and Expressions of True Religion.

First we cite the duty of prayer. Clearly we are not asked to perform this duty in order to declare God's perfections, His majesty, holiness, goodness, and all sufficiency. Our meanness, emptiness, dependence, and unworthiness show how unworthy we are, as do all our wants and desires. But He calls on us to pray in order to affect our hearts with the things we express and so to prepare us to receive the blessings that we ask. These gestures and behavior in our worship of God, in humility and reverence, have a tendency to affect our hearts as well as the hearts of others.

Prayer is a duty.

The duty of singing praises to God seems to be given wholly to excite and express religious affections. There is no other reason why we should express ourselves to God in verse rather than in prose and with music, except that these things have a tendency to move our affections.

Praise is a duty.

The sacraments are to nurture our affections.

We see this illustrated in the sacraments God has appointed. In considering our frame, God not only appointed that we should be told the great things of the gospel and of the redemption in Christ, but He also has instructed us by His Word. He has therefore given us sensible representations in the sacraments in order for them to affect us all the more.

The Word of God quickens and nurtures our affections.

This impression of divine things upon the hearts and affections of mankind is evidently one of the great and chief ways which God has ordained His Word to be delivered to mankind. His aim in the gift of the Scriptures is not that we should merely have good commentaries and expositions and other good books of theology. Although these may help us to have good understanding of the Word of God, they do not have as great a tendency to impress our hearts and affections. In preaching, God has appointed a particular and effective application of His Word to man. This He deems a fit way of affecting sinners with the importance of faith and of their need for remedy. The glory and the sufficiency of His provision is thus emphasized by preaching. He uses this also to stir up the pure minds of the saints, and to quicken their affections by often bringing the great things of true religion to their remembrance. In this way He sets before them the proper context of such full instruction (2 Peter 1:12, 13).

The two affections of love and joy are emphasized by Christ when He "gave some, apostles; and some, prophets; and some, evangelists; and some, pastors and teachers; that the Body of Christ might be edified in love" (Ephesians 4:11, 12, 16). The Apostle, in instructing and counseling Timothy concerning the work of the ministry, informs him that the great end of the Word is love and is to be preached (1 Timothy 1:3-5). God has also used preaching to promote joy in the saints. Therefore ministers are called "helpers of their joy" (2 Corinthians 1:24).

10. Hardness of Heart Is Sin.

Holiness of heart or true religion lies very much in the affections of the heart. And so the Scriptures consistently refer to hardness of heart as being the sin of the heart. Christ felt grief and displeasure toward the Jews because of the hardness of their hearts. "He looked round about on them with anger, being grieved for the hardness of their hearts" (Mark 3:5). Men brought wrath upon themselves because of their hearts. "After your hardness and impenitent heart, you treasure up to yourself wrath against the day of wrath, and the revelation of the righteous judgment of God" (Romans 2:5). Because they were hardhearted, the House of Israel would not obey God. "But the House of Israel will not hearken unto You. For they will not hearken unto me. For all the House of Israel are impudent and hard-hearted" (Ezekiel 3:7). The wickedness and rebellion of the generation in the wilderness is ascribed to the hardness of their hearts (Psalm 95:7-10). Hardness of heart prevented Zedekiah's turning to the Lord. "He stiffened his neck, and hardened his heart from turning to the Lord God of Israel" (2 Chronicles 36:13). When men rejected Christ and opposed Christianity, the same principle is mentioned: "But when divers were hardened, and believed not, but spoke evil of that way before the multitude" (Acts 19:9).

A hard heart is rebellious.

God has sometimes left man to the power of sin and the corruption of his heart. This is often expressed by God's hardening of hearts. "Therefore has He mercy on whom He will have mercy, and whom He wills He hardens" (Romans 9:18). "He has blinded their eyes, and hardened their hearts" (John 12:40). The Apostle seems to speak of "an evil heart that departs from the living God," and a "hard heart" as the same thing. "Harden not your heart, as in the provocation" (Hebrews 3:8, cf. 3:12, 13). The great work of God in conversion or the deliverance of a person from the power of sin is also expressed in this way. It is God's "taking away the heart of stone and giving a heart of flesh" (Ezekiel 11:19; 36:26).

A hard heart clearly implies an unaffected heart, or a heart that is not readily moved with virtuous affections. Like a stone, it is insensible, stupid, unmoved, and hard to impress. Hence a hard heart is called a stony heart, as opposed to a heart of flesh that has feelings and is sensibly touched and moved. We read in Scripture of a hard heart and a tender heart. Doubtless we are to view these as opportunities.

Is not a tender heart easily impressed with what ought to affect it? God commends Josiah because his heart was tender: "Because your heart was tender, and you have humbled yourself before the Lord, when you heard what I spoke in this place and against the inhabitants thereof, that they should become a desolation and a curse, you have rent your clothes, and wept before me. So I also have heard you, says the Lord" (2 Kings 22:19). Like little children we should have our hearts tender and easily affected and moved in spiritual and divine things.

It is very clear from other texts that hardness of heart means the heart that is void of affection. We are told the ostrich has no natural affection for her young, "she hardens her heart against her young ones, as though they were not hers" (Job 39:16). Similarly, a person whose heart is unaffected by danger is also described as hardening his heart. "Happy is the man that always fears; but he that hardens his heart shall fall into mischief" (Proverbs 28:14).

Since Scripture clearly implies by a hard heart someone who is destitute of pious affections, we can understand the frequent connection between this and the sins and corruptions of the heart. In contrast, it is also clear that the grace and holiness of the heart result largely from having pious affection and from being readily susceptible of such affection. Scholars generally agree that sin radically and fundamentally consists in what is negative and what deprives one of the very basis of holiness. If sin consists so much of the hardness of heart and lacks pious affections, then clearly holiness consists very much in the possession of such pious affections.

But I am far from suggesting that all affections show a tender heart. For hatred, anger, pride, and other selfish and self-exalting affections may greatly prevail in the hardest of hearts. Clearly, hardness of heart and tenderness of heart are expressions that relate to the emotions and denote what the heart is susceptible of or shut up against. I shall speak more about this later.

CONCLUDING INFERENCES

So generally, I think it is clear and abundantly evident that true religion lies very much in the affections. It is not that these arguments prove religion in the hearts of the truly godly is ever exactly proportionate to the amount of affection. For undoubtedly there is much emotion in the true saints which is not spiritual. Their religious affections are often mixed. All is not from grace, for much is from nature. While the affections do not originate in the body, yet the bodily state may contribute much to their present state of emotion. So the degree of religious life may be judged by the fixity and strength of habit that is exercised in affection. The strength of such a habit is not always in proportion to outward effects and evidences. But it is obvious that religion consists so much of affection, that without holy affection there can be no real, faithful heart. There can be no light in the understanding that is good, which does not produce holy, heartfelt affection.

Thus having considered the evidence of this proposition, let me proceed with some inferences.

First, recognize how grave is the error of discarding all religious affections as having nothing solid or substantial about them. This seems to be very common today. It may be a reaction against many during the great Revival who exaggerated the intensity of their emotions and the heat of their zeal. When others saw that their intense emotions came to nothing, they reacted and went from one extreme to another. Three or four years ago such affections were much in vogue, but they brought all religion into disrepute. They were, in reality, nothing at all.

Wrong affection does not mean we should not have affections.

But those without any religious affection are in a state of spiritual death. They are wholly destitute of the powerful, quickening, saving influences of the Spirit of God upon their hearts. So while it is true that where there is nothing but emotionalism there can be no true religion, likewise there can be no true religion where there is no religious affection. There must be light in the understanding as well as the fervency of heart, for if a heart has heat without light, there can be nothing divine or heavenly in that heart. On the other hand, where there is light without heat, such as a head stored with notions and speculations but having a cold and unaffected heart, there can be nothing divine in that light either. Such knowledge is no true spiritual knowledge of divine things. If the great things of religion are rightly understood, they will affect the heart. So the reason men are not affected by such infinitely great, important, and glorious things as they often read in the Word of God is undoubtedly that they are blind.

To devalue all religious affections is the way to harden the hearts of men and to encourage them in their folly and senselessness. This keeps them in a state of spiritual death, as long as they go on living, and at last brings them to eternal death. So the prevailing prejudice against religious affections today has the awful effect of hardening the hearts of sinners, of dampening the grace of many saints, and of reducing all to a state of dullness and apathy. To despise and cry against all religious affections is a sure way of shutting all religion out of the heart and of ruining souls. Those who condemn such warm affections in others are certainly not likely to have it themselves. In summary, those who have little religious affection have very little religion.

Need to promote true affections

Second, if true religion lies much in the affections, then we should do as much as possible to stimulate the affections. Those kinds of books, types of preaching of the Word, and liturgies of worship that help us worship God in prayer and praises are to be encouraged, as they help to affect deeply the hearts of those who do these things. But in these times, the apathetic way in which prayer and preaching are practiced no longer excites the affections. Rather, it causes disgust and only creates displeasure and contempt.

Third, if true religion lies so much in the affections, we should realize, to our shame before God, that we are not more affected with the great things of faith. It appears from what we have said that this arises from our having so little true religion.

For God has given affections to man for the same purpose that He has given all the faculties of the human soul, namely that they might serve "man's chief end," which is the great business for which God has created him, namely the business of religion. Yet we find that people exercise the affections in everything else but religion! When it comes to their worldly interest, their outward delights, their honor and reputation, and their natural relations, they have warm affection and ardent zeal. In these things their hearts are tender and sensitive, easily moved, deeply impressed, much concerned, and much engrossed. They get deeply depressed at worldly losses, and highly excited at worldly successes. But how insensible and unmoved are most men about the great things of another world! How dull then are their affections! Here their love is cold, their desires languid, their zeal low, and their gratitude small. How can they sit and hear of the infinite height, depth, length, and breadth of the love of God in Christ Jesus, of His gift of His infinitely dear Son offered up as a sacrifice for the sins of men, and yet be so insensible and regardless! Can we suppose that the wise Creator implanted such a faculty of affections to be occupied in this way? How can any Christian who believes the truth of these things not realize this?

If the Creator has wisely made human nature in this manner, why then misuse our affections? Can we Christians find anything worthier to respond to with all our affections than what is set forth to us in the gospel of Jesus Christ? Can anything be worthier to affect us than this? For the glory and beauty of the blessed Lord shine in all

We need true affections to serve God.

their luster in the face of an incarnate, infinitely loving, meek, compassionate, and dying Redeemer. All the virtues of the Lamb of God such as humility, patience, meekness, submission, obedience, love, and compassion, are shown to us in such a way as to most deeply move our affections. We see too the awful effects of the nature of our sin which our Redeemer undertook and suffered for us. There we see in the most affecting way God's hatred of sin and His wrath and judgment. As we see His justice and His wrath, we realize what a dreadful punishment was borne for our sins. What cause then have we to be humbled in the dust, that we are not moved more than we are!

Part II
HOW THE RELIGIOUS AFFECTIONS MAY BE FALSELY APPRAISED

II
FALSE SIGNS OF TRUE RELIGIOUS AFFECTIONS

Someone, after reading what has just been said in the previous chapter, is likely to excuse himself and say, "I am not one of those who have no religious affections, for I am often deeply moved when I consider the great realities of religion." However, he should not assume that he has, indeed, religious affections. For just as we should not reject all affections as if real faith does not consist of them, we ought not to sanction them all, saying everyone that is religiously affected has true grace and is therefore subject to the saving influences of the Spirit of God. Let him therefore conclude from this that it is required to distinguish between one kind or another of religious affections. In discussing this further I want to do two things in the rest of this book.

1. I want to list those things which we cannot use as evidence when we judge the authenticity of affections. We need to guard against judging the affections by false evidence.

2. I want to observe some ways in which the affections are spiritual and gracious and how these differ from those which are not. I will also discuss how true affections may be distinguished and known.

First, then, in this chapter let us take note of some of the ways in which the true affections may be falsely appraised.

I. THE INTENSITY OF RELIGIOUS AFFECTIONS IS NO EVIDENCE

Some are ready to condemn all intense affections. They are immediately prejudiced when they see people raising their religious affections to a high pitch and, without further consideration, dismiss these affections as delusions. But if true religion lies deeply within the religious affections, then there will be great affections in a rich quality of true faith.

Love, for example, is an affection. Dare any Christian say that people ought not to love God and Jesus Christ intensely? Dare anyone say that we should not hate sin greatly and be much pained by it? Should we not be grateful to God for all His mercies we have received? Should we not desire to seek God and a holy life? Can anyone remain content with the *status quo* of his life, saying, "I do not need to be humbled, I am all right as I am." No one who has realized something of the love of Christ who died for us can remain indifferent. No one can really believe such affections for God can ever be the ruin of true religion.

Our text plainly speaks of great and high affections when it speaks of "rejoicing with joy unspeakable, and full of glory." Indeed, the most superlative expressions are used. Clearly the Scriptures often require us to exercise the most intense affections. In the first and great commandment of the Law there is an accumulation of expressions, as though words were not enough to express the degree to which we ought to love God. "You shall love the LORD your God with all your heart, with all your soul, with all your mind, and with all your strength" (Deuteronomy 6:5). The saints are called upon to exercise a high degree of joyfulness. "Rejoice," says Christ to His disciples, "and be exceeding glad" (Matthew 5:12, cf. Psalm 68:3). In the Psalms, the saints are often called upon to shout for joy. In Luke 6:23 they are exhorted "to leap for joy." The saints are called upon "to praise God with all their hearts, with hearts lifted up in the ways of the Lord, and their souls magnifying the Lord, to sing His praises, to talk of His wondrous works, and to declare His doings."

We find the most eminent saints in Scripture often professing intense affections. The Psalmist speaks of his love as if it were unspeakable: "O how I love Thy law!" (Psalm 119:97). Likewise, he expresses an intense hatred of sin: "Do not I hate them, O LORD, that hate You? And am I not grieved with them that rise up against You? I hate them with perfect hatred" (Psalm 139:21, 22). He also expresses an intense sorrow for sin. He speaks of his sins "going over his head like a heavy burden that was too heavy for him." He speaks "of his roaring all the day, and his moisture being turned into the drought of summer." He describes his bones as if they were broken with sorrow. He often expresses intense spiritual desires in a wide range of the strongest expressions conceivable. For example, he speaks of his longing, his soul's thirsting as in a dry and thirsty land where no water is and where his panting, his flesh and heart cry out because his soul is broken for the longing that it has. For the sins of others he expresses intense and extreme grief. "Rivers of water run down my eyes, because they keep not Your law" (Psalm 119:136). In verse 53, he says, "Horror has taken hold upon me because of the wicked that forsake Your law." He also expresses intense joy: "The king shall joy in Your strength, and in Your salvation how greatly shall he rejoice" (Psalm 21:1). "My lips shall greatly rejoice when I sing unto You" (Psalm 71:23). "Because Your loving kindness is better than life, my lips shall praise You. Thus I will bless You while I live: I will lift up my hands in Your name. My soul shall be satisfied as with marrow and fatness; and my mouth shall praise You with joyful lips, when I remember You upon my bed, and meditate on You in the night watches. Because You have been my help, therefore in the shadow of Your wings will I rejoice" (Psalm 63:3-7).

The Psalmist expresses intense affections.

The Apostle Paul expresses intense qualities of affection. To the point of anguish in his heart, he expresses pity and concern for others' good. He has a great, fervent, and abundant love, with earnest and longing desires, and he has exceeding joy. He speaks of the exaltation and the

The Apostle Paul expresses intense affections.

triumphs of his soul, of his earnest expectation and hope, of his abundant tears, and frequently of the travails of his soul in pity, grief, earnest desires, godly jealousy, and fervent zeal. Many of these have already been mentioned so I need not repeat them.

John the Baptist does likewise.

Similarly, John the Baptist expresses great joy (John 3:29). Also, those blessed women who anointed the body of Jesus are represented as exercising intense affections at Christ's resurrection. "They departed from the sepulchre with fear and great joy" (Matthew 28:8).

The Church will express great affections.

It is often foretold that the Church of God, in her future happy state on earth, will rejoice exceedingly. "They shall walk, O LORD, in the light of Your countenance. In Your name shall they rejoice all the day: and in Your righteousness shall they be exalted" (Psalm 89:15, 16, cf. Zechariah 9:9). Indeed, since much joy is the true fruit of the gospel of Christ, the angel calls this gospel "good tidings of great joy, that shall be to all people."

The saints and angels in heaven in all their perfection are exceedingly affected when they behold and contemplate the perfection of God's works. Their love is as a pure heavenly flame of fire, as is the greatness and strength of their joy and gratitude. Their praises are represented as the voice of many waters and as the voice of a great thunder. For they respond perfectly to the greatness of God's love.

These examples show that religious affections are intense. To condemn people for being enthusiasts and to assume that their affections are only emotional is a great error.

True affections are not necessarily intense.

On the other hand, intensity is no evidence of true religious affections. For it is very clear from Holy Scripture, which is our sure and infallible rule for guidance, that intense affections may not be spiritual and saving. The Apostle Paul fears that the exalted affections of the Galatians had been exercised in vain and so came to nothing. He asks, "Where is the blessedness you spoke of? For I bear you record, that if it had been possible you would have plucked out your own eyes, and given them to me" (Galatians 4:15). In the eleventh verse he tells them he was afraid for them, lest he had bestowed upon them labor in vain. Similarly, the children of Israel were greatly affected with God's mercy on them when they saw how wonderfully He intervened for them at the Red Sea, and they sang God's praise. However, they soon forgot His works. They were greatly affected again at Mount Sinai when they saw the marvelous manifestations God made of Himself there. Confidently they responded: "All that the Lord has spoken will we do, and be obedient." But how soon their enthusiasm and show of affection ended! How quickly they turned aside after other gods, rejoicing and shouting around their golden calf!

According to Evangelist John, great multitudes were affected by the miracle of raising Lazarus from the dead (John 12:18). What a to-do the crowd made when Jesus entered Jerusalem. Cutting the branches of palm trees and scattering them in the way, they exalted Christ as though the ground beneath Him was not good enough for the ass that He rode upon. Indeed, they pulled off their garments and spread them in the way, crying with loud voices, "Hosanna to the Son of David. Blessed is He that comes in the name of the Lord, Hosanna in the highest" (Matthew 21:8, 9). It was as if the whole city rang again, putting all into an uproar. Here was a vast multitude crying "Hosanna," and this gave occasion for the Pharisees to say, "Behold, the world has gone after Him" (John 12:19). However, at that time Christ had only a few true disciples. And how quickly all this celebration came to an end! It was all quelled and dead when the same Jesus stood bound, with a mock robe and a crown of thorns, to be derided, spit upon, scourged, condemned, and executed. Indeed, there was a great and loud outcry concerning Him among the multitude then, as there was before. But it was of a very different kind. No longer was it "Hosanna, Hosanna," but "Crucify, crucify!"

True affections are sustained.

All Orthodox thinkers concur that religious affections may be raised to an intense pitch, but this is no evidence of true religion.[1]

II. BODILY AFFECTIONS ARE NO EVIDENCE OF TRUE AFFECTIONS

In some way or other, all affections do have an effect upon the body. As we have seen already, the nature of the union of body and soul is such that all lively and vigorous effects on the mind influence the body. But intense bodily reactions are not evidence that the affections are spiritual.

True affections may affect us bodily. On the other hand, I do not know of any standard which can prove that gracious and holy affections will not have a great effect on the body. I see no reason why the experience of God's glory might not cause the body to faint. There is a great power in spiritual affections; we read of the power which works in Christians (Ephesians 3:7), and of the Spirit of God being within them as a Spirit of power (2 Timothy 1:7), and of the effectual working of His power in them (Ephesians 3:7, 20). In contrast, man's nature is weak. Flesh and blood are represented in Scripture as exceedingly weak and are described particularly as being unfit for great spiritual and heavenly operations and exercises (Matthew 26:41; 1 Corinthians 15:43, 50).

The text we are discussing refers to "joy unspeakable, and full of glory." When one considers man's nature and the nature of his affections, he cannot help seeing that such unutterable and glorious joys may be too great and overwhelming for the weak dust and ashes of our human condition. Indeed, no man can see God and live.

Speaking of his intense religious emotions, the Psalmist refers to the effect they had upon his flesh or body, as well as upon his soul. "My soul longs, yea, even faints for

---

[1]Mr. Stoddard observes, "Common motions are sometimes stronger than saving ones," *Guide to Christ*, p. 21.

the courts of the Lord: my heart and my flesh cry out for the living God" (Psalm 84:2). Here a plain distinction is made between the heart and the flesh. Likewise in Psalm 63:1: "My soul thirsts for You, my flesh longs for You in a dry and thirsty land, where no water is."

The prophet Habakkuk speaks of his body being overwhelmed by the sense of the majesty of God. "When I heard, my belly trembled: my lips quivered at the voice: rottenness entered into my bones and I trembled in myself" (Habakkuk 3:16). The Psalmist also speaks specifically of his flesh trembling. "My flesh trembles for fear of You" (Psalm 119:120).

It is evident from Scripture that the ideas of God's glory that are sometimes given within this world have a tendency to overwhelm the body. For example, we have descriptions of this concerning the prophet Daniel and the Apostle John. Daniel said: "There remains no strength in me; for my comeliness is turned into corruption and I retain no strength" (Daniel 10:8). The Apostle John, giving an account of the revelation made to him, says: "And when I saw Him, I fell at His feet as dead" (Revelation 1:17). Consequently, they were greatly affected, their souls were swallowed up, and their bodies overwhelmed by the experience of God's presence and glory. They are rash, I think, who argue that God cannot and will not give similar experiences of the glory and majesty of His nature to any of His saints, without need of any such external shadows of it.

Before I leave this subject, let me observe that Scripture often plainly makes use of bodily effects in expressing the strength of holy and spiritual affections: "trembling" (Psalm 119:120; Ezra 9:4; Isaiah 66:2, 5; Habakkuk 3:16), "groaning" (Romans 8:26), being "sick" (Song of Solomon 2:5; 5:8), "crying out" (Psalm 84:2), "panting" (Psalm 38:10; 42:1; 119:131), and "fainting" (Psalm 84:2; 119:81). It may be argued that these are used as figurative expressions in order to represent the degree of affection. But I hope all will agree that they are fit and suitable

Bodily metaphors are used to express true affections.

figures which the Spirit of God makes use of to represent the intense experience of these spiritual affections. I cannot believe that the experience of such emotions could be mistaken for the false affections and delusions of the devil.

III. MUCH FLUENT AND FERVENT TALK IS NO EVIDENCE

There are many people who are greatly prejudiced against fluent and fervent talk in others. They will condemn those who are full of talk as Pharisees and ostentatious hypocrites. On the other hand, there are many who, when they see these talkers, immediately believe, ignorantly and foolishly, that they are true children of God and are under the saving influences of His Spirit. They speak of this talkativeness as great evidence of being new creatures. They argue that "such a person's mouth is now opened; he used to be slow to speak but now he is full and free. He is free to open his heart and declare the praises of God as freely as water from a fountain." And so on. But they are overconfident from this evidence.

Their conclusion shows little judgment and is but an ephemeral experience as events abundantly show later. It is a mistake for such people to trust their own wisdom and discernment instead of the Holy Scripture. For although the Scripture is full of rules, both how we should judge our own state and also how we should conduct ourselves before others, there are no rules by which to judge emotions.

Is it good to talk much about our religious experiences? People are inclined to talk much about religion. This may be from either a good cause or a bad cause. Their hearts may be very full of holy affections. "For out of the abundance of the heart the mouth speaks" (Matthew 12:34). But then again, it may be because people's hearts are full of religious affections which are not holy.

It all depends upon the nature of the affections. Such was the enthusiasm of the crowds that flocked to John the Baptist and to Jesus. It simply meant they were moved emotionally, only ephemerally so.

So a person may be full of talk about his own experiences. But often it is more a bad than a good sign. It is like a tree that is full of leaves that seldom bears much fruit. Or it is like a cloud which, although it appears to promise much fullness of rain, is only wind to a dry and thirsty earth. The Holy Spirit often uses this symbol to represent the mere verbal exhibition of religion, which has no answerable truth in the life. "Whoso boasts himself of a false gift, is like clouds and wind without rain" (Proverbs 25:14).

Too much talk is a bad sign.

Strong, false affections are much more likely to declare themselves than true ones. It is the nature of false religion to be showy and visible, as it was with the Pharisees.[2]

IV. IMPOSED EMOTIONS ARE NOT EVIDENCE

There are many these days that condemn all stimulated affections that cannot be explained. These affections do not seem to be a result of their own efforts, nor the natural consequence of their own faculties. Somehow they seem to be influenced by some external and supernatural power upon their minds. How greatly has the doctrine of the inward experience, or the sensible perception of the immediate power and operation of the Spirit of God been reproached and ridiculed by many recently! They argue that the Spirit of God cooperates in a silent, secret, and undiscernible manner, through our own efforts. So no distinction is made between the influences of the Spirit of God and the natural operation of our own mental faculties.

It is an unreasonable presumption for anyone to expect to receive the saving influences of the Spirit of God while

---

[2]The distinguished pastoral theologian, Thomas Shepard, says, "A Pharisee's trumpet shall be heard to the end of the town but simplicity walks through the town unseen" (*Parable of the Ten Virgins*, part 1, p. 179). The saintly John Flavel says: "Religion does not lie open to all the eyes of men. Observed duties maintain our credit; but secret duties maintain our life. They are enclosed pleasures in religion, which none but renewed spiritual souls do feelingly understand (*Touchstone of Sincerity*, chapter 2, section 2, p. 21).

he neglects a diligent improvement of the means appointed by grace. To expect that the Spirit of God will operate savingly upon their minds without making use of means is too emotional. It is also undoubtedly true that the Spirit of God uses diverse means and circumstances, and at times He operates in a more secret and gradual way, and from smaller beginnings, than at other times.

God's favor is bound to affect us radically.

But if there is indeed a power that is entirely different from and beyond our power, then is it unreasonable to suppose that this may be produced externally? If grace indeed is powerful and efficacious of some external agent, or if divine power is outside of ourselves, why is it unreasonable to suppose that it can and will operate in such subjects? Is it as strange as it appears to be? When grace in the heart is not produced by our strength, nor as a result of our natural faculties, nor produced by any means or instruments other than the consequence of the Spirit of the Almighty, is it strange and unaccountable that this should happen?

The Scripture abundantly teaches that grace in the soul is so affected by God's power that it may be aptly compared to new birth, or a resurrection or creation, or being brought out of nothing. These metaphors are used to illustrate the mighty power of God that is so greatly glorified and exceedingly marvelous to behold (Ephesians 1:17-20).

But God may also affect us secretly.

But what of those instances where it appears that the Almighty performs such great works secretly? What is the reason for this? If we may judge from the Scripture, it appears He does act often inconspicuously so that man's dependence upon Him might be made more evident, and that no flesh should glory in His presence (1 Corinthians 1:27-29). He does it also that God alone might be exalted (Isaiah 2:1-17) and that "the excellency of the power might be of God and not of man" (2 Corinthians 4:7). That is how Christ's power is made manifest in our weakness (2 Corinthians 12:9). He declares that none but His hand has saved me (Judges 7:7).

Gideon's men and David before Goliath illustrate this same principle. The gospel has always confounded the philosophers of this world.

The Apostle in Ephesians 1:18, 19 speaks of God's enlightening the minds of Christians and thereby bringing them to believe in Christ. The purpose is that they might know the exceeding greatness of His power to them who believe. The exact words are:

> The eyes of your understanding being enlightened; that you may know what is the hope of His calling, and what the riches of the glory of His inheritance in the saints, and what is the exceeding greatness of His power to us-ward who believe, according to the working of His mighty power.

God enlightens the mind.

Now when the Apostle speaks of their being subject to God's power in their enlightenment and effectual calling, he shows that the whole purpose of this is nothing else than "that they might know it personally by experience." If the saints know this power experientially, then they feel it and consciously discern it as distinguishable from the natural operations of their own minds. Their own minds are not agreeable to God's operating so secretly and undiscernibly that it cannot be demonstrated that they are subject to any extrinsic power at all.

It is very unreasonable and unscriptural, then, to determine that the affections are not from God's Spirit because they are not from the persons themselves.

However, it is no evidence that affections are of God when they are not properly produced by those who are subjects of them, or when they arise in their minds in a way that is unaccountable.

Inexplicable emotions are not necessarily of God.

There are some who make this an argument in their own favor. When speaking of what they have experienced, they say: "I am sure that I did not make it up myself. It was not the fruit of any contrivance or endeavor of my own. When it came I was not thinking about it. If I were given the whole world for it, I could not repeat it when I liked." So they believe that what they have experienced must be from the Spirit of God, and therefore it must be of saving value. They do so ignorantly and without good reason. For it may be some other spirit. But it does not follow that it is the Holy Spirit. So we are exhorted to test the spirits.

People may also have impressions on their minds which were not produced by themselves, nor were they produced by an evil spirit, but rather by the Spirit of God. Yet these may have no saving value but only be a common influence of the Spirit of God. Such may be the experience of those whom we read of in Hebrews 6:4, 5: "That are once enlightened, and taste of the heavenly gift, and made partakers of the Holy Ghost, and taste the good word of God, and the power of the world to come." Yet still they may be wholly unacquainted with those "better things that accompany salvation" (v. 9).

V. SCRIPTURE TESTS

The experience of Scripture being brought to the mind is no evidence of gracious affections. The truth of Scripture certainly contains and teaches what is the foundation of true affections, but the mere sudden and unusual remembrance of Scripture does not.

Emotional reactions to Scripture are not enough. Emotional reactions to the Scriptures, whether of fear, hope, joy, sorrow, or any other, may not themselves be evidence of a genuine experience. There are some who think that their emotions have saving value, especially if these emotions move them to have hope or joy or to enjoy anything else that is pleasurable or delightful. They will cite this as evidence that all is well, and that their experience must have come from the Word. So they will argue, "There were such and such sweet promises that came to my mind. They came suddenly as if they were spoken to me personally. I had no hand in bringing such a text to my mind."

What deceives unreflective people such as this is the following type of argument. Scripture is the Word of God and so it is inerrant; therefore those experiences which come from Scripture must always be right. But we should remember that emotions may arise on occasion from the Scripture that do not arise from the Scriptures as a genuine fruit of the Scriptures, but only emotionally so. These emotions abuse the Scriptures. It is therefore false to assume that since I had certain feelings while reading the Scriptures, these feelings must be all right. All that can be argued from the purity and perfection of the Word of God regarding experiences such as these is that those experiences which are agreeable to the Word of God are right.

Is there not evidence that the devil can take texts of Scripture and misapply them in order to deceive people? This is certainly within the power of Satan. It is no great thing to bring sounds or letters to people's minds, and if Satan has power to do this, he also has the power to bring words that are contained in the Bible. It is no greater thing for emotions to arise out of a text of Scripture than out of any idle story or song. Are texts of Scriptures such sacred things that the devil dare not abuse or touch them? Did he not boldly challenge Christ Himself in the wilderness, taking Him hither and thither, to a high mountain and to the pinnacle of the temple? He is not afraid to touch the Scripture and to abuse it for his own purpose. Indeed, he brought one Scripture after another to Christ in order to deceive and to tempt Him. Can he not then go on attempting to deceive people today with texts of Scripture? He may heap up Scripture promises and apply them perversely, using them to remove rising doubts, or to confirm false joy and confidence in a poor, deluded sinner.

The devil, too, can use Scripture.

Likewise, corrupt and false teachers can, and do, pervert the Scripture to their own and to others' destruction (2 Peter 3:16). We see how they make free use of Scripture so that there is no text too precious or sacred that they

False teachers can also use the Scriptures.

are not allowed to abuse to the eternal ruin of multitudes. Man's heart is deceitful, like the devil, and man uses the same means to deceive.

It is clear that anyone can have experiences of intense affections such as hope and joy from reading texts of Scripture. Indeed, precious promises from the Bible can come suddenly and remarkably to the mind in a wonderful sequence and as though they were actually spoken. Yet none of this is sufficient argument that these affections are divinely inspired; indeed, they may be the effects of Satan's delusions.

The Scriptures can arouse false emotions.

I would further observe that people may be aroused to joyful affections which may come from the Word of God and even indicate some influence of the Spirit of God, and yet there is still nothing of the nature of true and saving religion in such experiences. Thus, in the parable of the sower, there were those hearers likened to stony ground that heard the Word with great joy; indeed, there was some growth in the seed. Their affections had the appearance of the true plants that grew on the good soil. It was only later, in a time of testing, that the difference between the two became noticeable. Then it became evident that there was no saving religion in these affections.[3]

VI. THE EXHIBITION OF LOVE IS NO EVIDENCE OF TRUE RELIGIOUS AFFECTIONS

Many suppose that to have love is a good evidence that such affections are the sanctifying and saving influences of the Holy Spirit. They argue that Satan cannot love. Since love is contrary to the devil whose nature is enmity and

---

[3]Mr. Stoddard in his *Guide to Christ* (1735) speaks of it as a common occurrence for people before they have ever accepted Christ to have in a natural way Scripture promises come to them with a great deal of refreshment. They take these as tokens of God's love, and hope that God has accepted them; and so they are confident of their true condition (pp. 8, 9).

malice, all love must be truly Christian. After all, is such love not more excellent than knowledge, prophecy, miracles, or even speaking with the tongues of men and of angels? Surely it is the chief of the graces of God's Spirit, as well as the life, essence, and sum of all true religion. It is by this that we are most conformed to heaven and most in contrast to hell and the devil.

But this is a poor argument, for it assumes that there are no counterfeits of love. It should always be noted that the more excellent something is, the more likely it will be imitated. Thus there are more counterfeits of silver and gold than of iron and copper. There are many false diamonds and rubies, but who goes about making counterfeit pebbles? However, the more excellent things are, the more difficult it is to imitate them in their essential character and intrinsic virtues. Yet the more varied will the imitations be, the more skill and subtlety will be used in making them an exact imitation, at least of the outward appearance. So it is with Christian virtues and graces. The devil and men's own deceitful hearts tend to imitate those things that have the highest value. So no graces are more counterfeited than love and humility. For these are the virtues where the beauty of a true Christian is seen most clearly.

Only valuables are counterfeited.

It is plain from the Scriptures that a person may have a kind of religious love, and yet have no saving grace. Christ speaks of many professing Christians that have such love, but whose love will not continue and so it will lack salvation. "And because iniquity shall abound, the love of many shall wax cold. But he that shall endure unto the end, the same shall be saved" (Matthew 24:12, 13). These words plainly show that those whose love will not endure to the end will not be saved.

People may seem to have love for God and Christ, even strong and intense affections of this nature, and yet have no grace. This was the case with many graceless Jews, who followed Jesus day and night, even without food or sleep.

A show of love is not enough.

Such said, "Lord, I will follow You wherever You go," and cried, "Hosanna to the Son of David."[4]

The Apostle seems to intimate that there were many in his own day who had a counterfeit love for Christ. "Grace be with all them that love our Lord Jesus Christ in sincerity" (Ephesians 6:24). The last word in the Greek signifies "incorruption," showing that the Apostle was aware that there were many who had a kind of love for Christ which was not pure or spiritual.

So Christian love for the people of God may also be counterfeited. It is evident from the Scriptures that there may be strong affections of this kind without saving grace as there was with the Galatians toward the Apostle Paul. They said they were ready to pluck out their eyes and give them to him. Yet the Apostle expresses his fear that their affections would come to nothing and that he had labored in vain for them (Galatians 4:11, 15).

VII. MANY ACCOMPANYING KINDS OF RELIGIOUS AFFECTIONS ARE NOT EVIDENCE ENOUGH

Although pseudoreligion is apt to be absurd and unbalanced when compared with true religion, it may still contain a great variety of false affections that resemble the true ones.

It is clear that there are counterfeits of all kinds of gracious affections both with regard to the love of God, as well as to the love of brethren, as we have just noted. So we find there was an exercise of godly sorrow for sin in the case of Pharaoh, Saul, Ahab, and the children of Israel in the wilderness (Exodus 9:27; 1 Samuel 24:16, 17; 26:21; 1 Kings 21:27; Numbers 14:39, 40). There is reference to the fear of God in the Samaritans "who feared the LORD, and served their own god at the same time" (2 Kings 17:32, 33). We read of enemies of God who "through the greatness of God's power, submit themselves to Him"

---

[4]Stoddard, *Guide to Christ*, pp. 21-65.

(Psalm 66:3), or as it is in the Hebrew, "lie unto Him." In other words, they give a counterfeit reverence and submission. We read also of the expression of gracious gratitude in the children of Israel when they sang God's praise at the Red Sea (Psalm 106:12) and in Naaman the Syrian after his miraculous healing of leprosy (2 Kings 5:15).

We can cite examples of the experience of spiritual joy in those hearers that were like stony ground (Matthew 13:20), and particularly in many of John the Baptist's hearers (John 5:35). We hear also of zeal exercised in this way by Jehu (2 Kings 10:16) and in Paul before his conversion (Galatians 1:14; Philippians 3:6). Likewise, we hear of unbelieving Jews having zeal (Acts 22:3; Romans 10:2). So people without the grace of God may exercise intense religious desires such as those Baalam exercised (Numbers 23:9, 10). They may also have, like the Pharisees, a strong hope of eternal life.

False affections may be very varied.

If, then, the natural man is capable of having a resemblance of all kinds of religious affections, nothing will hinder him from having a number of them together. Indeed this often happens. And when such false affections are exercised intensely, many of them associate together.

VIII. The Resultant Comfort and Joys That Follow Spiritual Awakening and Conviction of Conscience Are Not Evidence

Many people seem prejudiced against experiences and affections that come in a dramatic way, for example, when awakenings, fears, and awful apprehensions come from humble beginnings such as a sense of total depravity and helplessness in sin, and then are followed by some light and comfort. Some scholars question all such techniques and steps that may be outlined for men to follow. They may be particularly skeptical if an intense experience of joy follows a great sense of distress and terror.

Intense emotional
experiences are
not necessarily
suspect.

But such objections and prejudices are without reason or indeed scriptural backing. For surely it is not unreasonable to expect that when God delivers some people from a state of sin and its destructive influence, He can give them an intense experience of the evil that He has delivered them from. In this way they may truly understand that they have been saved and have seen something of what God has done for them. When they have this deep experience of need, they can more properly experience the sufficiency of Christ and of God's mercy working in Him.

So it is God's way of dealing with mankind to lead them into a wilderness before He speaks comfortably to them. The principle that is many times demonstrated in Scripture is this: God will bring people into distress in order to make them see their own utter helplessness and absolute dependence upon His power and grace before He appears to work any great deliverance for them (Deuteronomy 32:36, 37).

Before God delivered the children of Israel out of Egypt, He prepared them for it by making them see that they were in a difficult situation, and "cry unto God, because of their hard bondage" (Exodus 2:23; 5:19).

Likewise, before God gave them the great deliverance at the Red Sea, they were brought into great distress. The wilderness had shut them in, they could turn neither to the right hand nor to the left, and the Red Sea was before them. Behind them was the great Egyptian host. They were brought to see that they could do nothing to help themselves. If God did not help them, they would be utterly destroyed. It was then that God appeared, and turned their cries into songs. So before they were brought to their rest, to enjoy the milk and honey of Canaan, God "led them through a great and terrible wilderness, that He might humble them and teach them what was in their heart, and so do them good in their latter end" (Deuteronomy 8:2, 16).

The woman who had the issue of blood twelve years was not cured until she had first "spent all her livelihood on earthly physicians, and could not be healed of any" and so was left helpless, without any more money to spend. Then she came to the great Physician and was healed by Him without charge (Luke 8:43, 44). Before Christ would answer the request of the woman of Canaan, He appeared first to deny her totally, to humble her, and to bring her to see that she was not more worthy than to be called a dog. Then He showed her mercy, and received her as a dear child (Matthew 15:22, ff.).

Likewise we read of a time when the disciples and Jesus were on a ship in the middle of a great tempest. The disciples, fearful of perishing, cried to Jesus: "Lord, save us. We perish." Then the winds and the seas were rebuked and there was a great calm (Matthew 8:24-26). The Apostle Paul, before a remarkable deliverance, was "pressed out of measure, above strength, so much that he despaired even of life; he had the sentence of death in himself, that he might not trust in himself, but in God that raises the dead" (2 Corinthians 8, 9).

If we then consider the wonderful revelations which God made of Himself to the saints of old, we will find that He commonly first reveals Himself in a way which is terrible, and then later by those things that are assuring and comforting. This was true with Abraham. First the horror of a great darkness fell upon him, and then God revealed Himself to him in sweet promises (Genesis 15:12, 13). It was true with Moses at Mt. Sinai. First, God appeared to him in all the terrors of His dreadful Majesty, so that Moses said: "I exceedingly fear and quake." Then God made all His goodness to pass before him, and proclaimed His name, "The Lord God, gracious and merciful." With Elijah there was first a stormy wind, earthquake, and devouring fire, and then came a still, small voice (1 Kings 19). Daniel saw Christ's countenance as lightning which terrified him and caused him to swoon. Then he was strengthened and refreshed with comforting words such as these: "O Daniel, a man greatly beloved" (Daniel 10). Again it was true with the Apostle John (Revelation 1).

There are many passages of Scripture which show that God first brings man face to face with his own depravity

God may first appear terrifying before He comforts.

and then He reveals His grace. The servant that owed his master ten thousand pounds is first held to his debt and the king pronounces a sentence of condemnation upon him. He commands him to be sold, with his wife and children, and full payment to be made. Thus He humbles him, and brings him to agree that the whole of his debt is just. Then He forgives him completely. The prodigal son spends all that he has and is brought to humble himself and to see himself in destitution and to see his unworthiness before he is forgiven and then feasted by his father (Luke 15).

For God first exposes sin before He gives healing.

The old, original wounds must first be probed in their depth before there can be healing. The Scripture compares sin with the wound of the soul and says that an attempt to heal this wound without examining it first is vain and deceitful (Jeremiah 8:11). It is God's method to show men how awful their state is before He brings the comfort of deliverance and healing. The gospel must be revealed as bad news before it can be good news.

It is therefore not unreasonable to suppose that people should suffer deep distress and much mental apprehension when they see how great and manifold are their sins in the light of the infinite majesty of God, and of the awfulness of His eternal wrath. This is all the more apparent in the clear examples in Scripture of those who were brought to this great distress by such convictions before they received saving consolations. Thus the multitude at Jerusalem "were pricked in their heart, and said unto Peter, and the rest of the apostles, 'Men and brethren, what shall we do?'" The Apostle Paul trembled and was astonished before he was comforted. The jailer "called for a light, sprang in, and came trembling, and fell down before Paul and Silas, saying, 'Sirs, what must I do to be saved?'"

From this evidence it appears to be very reasonable for professing Christians to object to the truth and spiritual nature of comfortable and joyful affections when they come after such awful apprehensions and distresses as have been mentioned.

On the other hand, it is no evidence that comforts and joys are right simply because they follow after great terrors, and paralyzing fears of hell.[5] Some teachers greatly emphasize the need to terrify people as evidence of the great work of the law that is wrought in the heart in order to prepare the way for solid comfort. But they forget that terror and a conviction of conscience are not the same thing. Although convictions of conscience do cause terror, they do not consist in it. Terrors do arise from other causes. Convictions of conscience, through the influence of God's Spirit, consist in convictions of simpleness of heart and practice. It is a conviction of the dreadfulness of sin as committed before a God of terrible majesty and infinite holiness who hates sin and exercises holy justice in punishing it. But there are some people who have frightful apprehensions of hell, yet they have very little true understanding of conscience. The devil, if permitted, can readily terrify men, as can the Spirit of God. It is a natural work for him to do, and he has many ways of doing it.

Yet true comforts do not necessarily come after real terrors.

Also, the fears and terrors that some people have are the result of their temperament. Their imaginations are more strongly impressed with everything they are affected with. And so the impression made on their imagination influences their affections and heightens them still further. Affection and imagination then act reciprocally, until the amplitude of their emotions is so great that they are totally swallowed up and possessed by them.[6]

Such emotions may be the result of personal temperament.

---

[5]Thomas Shepard speaks of "men being cast down as low as hell by sorrow and lying under chains, quaking in apprehension of terror to come, and then raised up to heaven and joy, not able to live; and yet not removed from lust, such are pitiful objects, and are like to be objects of terror at the great day" (*Parable of the Ten Virgins*, part 1, p. 175).

[6]The famous theologian, William Perkins, distinguishes between "those sorrows that come through convictions of conscience, and melancholic passions that arise from mere imagination, strongly conceived in the mind." This, he said, usually comes on suddenly, like a stroke of lightning upon a house (*Works*, vol. 1, p. 385).

So there are some people who speak of their wickedness who really have little or no conviction of sin. They speak of having a dreadfully hard heart, but they do not realize what this means. They talk of a dreadful load of conscience, like a heap of black and loathsome filth within them. Yet when the matter is looked into carefully, one sees that they have no idea what the corruption of nature really means, or how their own hearts are sinfully deceptive. Unfortunately, many think they have great convictions of their actual sins, and they describe how their sins are set before them and how these sins surround them with a dreadful appearance, and yet they really have no idea what the reality of sin is.

So just because people are afflicted with great terrors that appear to have been awakened and convinced by the Spirit of God, it does not necessarily follow that these terrors will lead to true comfort. The unmortified corruption of the heart may quench the Spirit of God after He has been striving to lead men away from their presumptuous and self-exalting hopes and joys. Not every woman in labor brings forth a healthy child. Sometimes the child can be deformed or mentally retarded. Thus we see that comforts and joys do not automatically come after there has been great terror and awakening. But these are no certain signs of the true and saving grace that should follow. There are four reasons for this.

The devil can counterfeit all emotions.

First of all, the devil can counterfeit all the saving operations and graces of the Spirit of God. He can also counterfeit those operations which are preparatory to the work of grace. Indeed, there are no works that are so sublime and divine and out of reach of all creatures that the devil cannot imitate them. Thus we read how Saul, wicked and proud, yet convinced of his sin, fell down with tears and wept before David, his subject whom he had mortally hated and openly treated as his enemy. He cried out: "You are more righteous than I: you have rewarded me good, whereas I have rewarded you evil!" On another occasion he confessed: "I have sinned, I have played the fool, I have erred exceedingly" (1 Samuel 24:16, 17; 26:21). Yet there seems to have been very little evidence of the influence of the Spirit of God in Saul's life. In fact, after God's Spirit had departed from him and given him up, an evil spirit from the Lord troubled him. If, then, this proud monarch in a pang of emotion was brought to humble himself before a subject whom he hated, yet afterwards still continued to pursue as an enemy, we, too, can appear to be under great conviction and humiliation before God, yet still remain His enemies.

The devil can be the counterfeit of God's Spirit.

Second, if the operations and effects of the Spirit of God in the convictions and comforts of true converts are sophisticated and yet can be imitated, then their order can also be imitated. If Satan can imitate the things themselves, he can easily change their sequence. However, Satan cannot *exactly* imitate divine operations in their nature. So a particular sequence is not necessarily reliable because it is the nature of the counterfeit to have no divine power that places experiences in their right order. And therefore no order or method of operations and experiences is any certain sign of their divinity.

We have no easy guide to the Holy Spirit's activities.

Third, we have no clear rule for determining how far God's Spirit may be operating in these convictions and emotions that are not truly spiritual and saving. There is no necessary connection in the nature of things between anything that a natural man may experience and the saving grace of God's Spirit. Only divine revelation can make this clear. God has revealed no clear connection between salvation and any qualification in man, except grace and its fruits. So we do not find any legal convictions or comforts as a sure method of evaluation. Never once are these referred to in Scripture as certain signs of grace or as things which are distinctive of the saints. But we do find gracious operations and their effects mentioned many thousands of times. This then should be enough for Christians who are willing to have the Word of God rather than their own philosophy or their own experiences and conjectures as a sufficient and sure guide.

Conversion experiences are not enough.

Fourth, experience greatly confirms that people who seem to have the right sequence of convictions and comforts do not necessarily have the grace of God.[7] So I appeal to all pastors in this country who have had occasion to deal with souls in this Revival movement, not just to believe in conversion stories but to see if there is clear evidence of the Spirit of God in such conversions. The steps taken and their sequence in such stories is no evidence of true conversion. Without the Spirit of God such techniques and methods mean nothing.

True conversion at first may be a confusing experience.

On the contrary, as Thomas Shepard observes, at first glance the work of change in a saint appears confused chaos. The saints do not know what to make of it, because the manner of the Spirit's proceeding in them is very often extremely mysterious and unsearchable. The mystery of the way of the Spirit in new birth is compared to our original birth in Ecclesiastes 11:5. "You do not know what is the way of the Spirit, or how the bones do grow in the womb of her that is with child: even so you do not know the works of God, who works all things."

The new creature may use the language of the Psalmist. "I am fearfully and wonderfully made; marvelous are Your works, and that my soul knows right well. My substance was not hid from You, when I was made in secret" (Psalm 139:14, 15). Of the birth of Christ, both in His own person and in the hearts of His people, it may be said in the words of Isaiah 53:8: "Who can declare his generation?" We do not know how God works. "It is the glory of God to conceal a thing" (Proverbs 25:2).

For God's ways are not our ways.

It is to be feared that some have gone too far in attempting to direct the Spirit of the Lord. Experience plainly

[7]Mr. Stoddard, who has had much experience of this, observed long ago that converted and unconverted men cannot be clearly distinguished by the account they may give of their own conversion. Many people have given a reasonable account of the work of conversion and have carried themselves in the eyes of the world for years, and still have not demonstrated the reality of their conversion (*Appeal to the Learned*, pp. 75, 76).

shows that God's Spirit is unsearchable and untraceable in the conversions of the best of Christians. The Spirit of God cannot be discerned as proceeding in a certain way. It may appear to us that a set procedure is necessary and that rules are established by common opinion, but this may falsify reality.

What we have chiefly to do with inquiries into our own state or in the directions we may give to others is to analyze the nature of the effect that God has brought to pass within the soul. The steps which the Spirit of God may have taken to bring things to pass must be left entirely to Him. In Scripture we are often directed to test whether the nature of our fruits are really of the Spirit. But nowhere is a description given of how His Spirit produces them.[8] So many greatly err in their notion of what is a clear evidence of conversion. They will describe it in terms of a sequence of steps and methods that are clear to them. However, the clearest work is the results of the spiritual and divine nature of the work done.

It is only by their fruits we really know.

IX. TRUE RELIGIOUS AFFECTIONS ARE NOT EQUATED WITH TIME AND EFFORT SPENT IN RELIGIOUS AFFECTIONS

It is common nowadays for people to argue unfairly against religious affections because of too much time spent reading, praying, singing, hearing sermons, and so on. But it is plain from the Scriptures that it is the tendency of true grace for people to delight in such religious exercises. True grace had this effect upon Anna, the prophetess (Luke 2:37). "She departed not from the temple, but served God with fastings and prayers night and day." Grace had this effect upon the early Christians in Jerusalem. "They continuing daily with one accord in the

True affections are active.

---

[8]"If a man does not know the time of his conversion, or when he first came to Christ, the minister cannot therefore draw any peremptory conclusion from this that he is not saved" (Stoddard, *Guide to Christ*, p. 83).

temple, and breaking bread from house to house, did eat their meat with gladness and singleness of heart, praising God" (Acts 2:46, 47). Grace made Daniel delight in the duty of prayer and to attend seriously to it three times a day. This was also true of David. "Evening, morning, and at noon will I pray" (Psalm 55:17). Indeed, grace makes the saints delight in singing praises to God. "Sing praises unto His name, for it is pleasant" (Psalm 135:3). "Praise you the Lord; for it is good to sing praises unto our God; for it is pleasant, and praise is comely" (Psalm 147:1).

Grace also causes them to delight in hearing the Word of God preached. The gospel is a joyful sound to them (Psalm 89:15). It makes the feet of those who publish these good tidings to be seen as beautiful. "How beautiful upon the mountains are the feet of him who brings good tidings!" (Isaiah 52:7). It makes them love the public worship of God. "Lord, I have loved the habitation of Your house, and the place where Your honor dwells" (Psalm 26:8). "One thing have I desired of the Lord, that will I seek after, that I may dwell in the house of the Lord all the days of my life, to behold the beauty of the Lord, and to inquire in His temple" (Psalm 27:4).

But true affections are not activism. This is the nature of true grace. But on the other hand, the zeal of the excessive worker could be simply a disposition of temperament and not necessarily any grace at all. This was so with the Israelites, whose services were abominable to God. They attended "the new moons and Sabbaths, and callings of assemblies, and spread forth their hands, and made many prayers" (Isaiah 1:12-15). This was also true with the Pharisees. "They made long prayers, and fasted twice a week." False religion may cause people to be loud and earnest in prayer. "You shall not fast as you do this day, to cause your voice to be heard on high" (Isaiah 58:4). Religion which is not spiritual and saving may motivate people to delight in religious duties and ordinances (see Isaiah 58:2; Ezekiel 33:31, 32).

So experience shows that people with false religion are apt to be exceedingly active in their religious activities.

Indeed, they may give themselves up to them and devote all their time to them.

X. VERBAL WORSHIP IS NO EVIDENCE OF TRUE RELIGIOUS AFFECTIONS

This indeed is implied in what we have just observed. To spend much time in external exercises of religion means nothing. So the fact that many appear to be greatly disposed to praying, to magnifying God, and to having their mouths full of His praise, does not mean very much.

No Christian will argue against someone's doing this. **Talk is not enough.** We are not in the habit of judging people who spend much time apparently in expressing such deep affections toward God and Christ, so that they are continually talking about Him. It is only when we look at Scripture that we will see this is no sure sign of grace.

We have already cited instances of this. A primary example is the multitude that was present when Christ preached and wrought miracles (Mark 2:12; Matthew 9:8; Luke 5:26). "The multitude wondered when they saw the dumb to speak, the maimed to be whole, the lame to walk, the blind to see: and they glorified the God of Israel" (Matthew 15:31). On one occasion when Christ raised the son of the widow of Nain, "there came a fear on all: and they glorified God, saying that a great prophet is risen up among us; and that God has visited His people" (Luke 7:16). We read of their glorifying Christ and speaking highly of Him. "He taught in their synagogues, being glorified of all" (Luke 4:15).

But again there is no certain evidence that a person has **Confession is not enough.** true affections simply because he is greatly affected by God's unmerited mercy. There may remain unmortified pride and enmity against God which he may even imagine he has received from God. He may cry out about his own worthlessness and yet have no real conviction of sin. Saul could confess, "I have played the fool, I have erred exceedingly" (1 Samuel 15:16-19; 26:21), and yet there still remained within him unsubdued pride and enmity against David. We read of Nebuchadnezzar and Darius, who were so affected by God's dealings that they called upon the nations to praise God (Daniel 3:28-30; 4:1-3, 34, 35, 37; 6:25-27).

XI. SELF-CONFIDENCE IS NO EVIDENCE OF TRUE AFFECTIONS

God's saints have confidence.

Some argue that people are deluded if they are so confident that they do not doubt the favor of God. They do not believe the church can expect a full and absolute assurance of hope except in such extraordinary circumstances as in the case of martyrdom. It is the criticism of many Protestants that Roman Catholics have this uncertainty.

On the other hand, the saints in the Scriptures do have this confidence. God in the plainest and most positive way revealed and testified His special favor to Noah, Abraham, Isaac, Jacob, Moses, Daniel, and others. Job often speaks of his sincerity and uprightness with the greatest confidence and assurance, often calling on God to witness to it. He says plainly, "I know that my Redeemer lives, and that I shall see Him for myself, and not another" (Job 19:25-27). Throughout the book of Psalms, David speaks almost without any hesitancy and in the most positive manner of God as his God. He glories in God as his portion and heritage, his rock and confidence, his shield, salvation, and high tower. Hezekiah appeals to God as one who knew that he walked before Him in truth and with a perfect heart (2 Kings 20:3).

Christ provides confidence.

In his dying discourse with His eleven disciples, Jesus Christ in the fourteenth, fifteenth, and sixteenth chapters of John, frequently declares His special and everlasting love to them in the plainest and most positive terms. In the most absolute manner, He promises them a future participation with Him in His glory. He tells them at the same time that He does this so that their joy might be full (John 15:11). Christ was not afraid of speaking too plainly and positively to them. He does not desire to hold them in suspense. He concludes His last discourse with a prayer in their presence in which He speaks positively to His Father of those eleven disciples as all knowing Him savingly, believing in Him, and having received and kept His Word.

Likewise the Apostle Paul, throughout his epistles, speaks with such assurance. He always speaks affirmatively of his special relationship to Christ, his Lord and Master and his Redeemer. He is confident of his future reward. It would be endless to cite all the places where his spirit of confidence is enumerated. Let me just mention three or four. "Christ lives in me, and the life which I now live in the flesh, I live by the faith of the Son of God, who loved me and gave Himself for me" (Galatians 2:20). "For me to live is Christ, and to die is gain" (Philippians 1:21). "I know whom I have believed, and am persuaded that He is able to keep that which I have committed unto Him against that day" (2 Timothy 1:12). "I have fought a good fight, I have finished my course, I have kept the faith. Henceforth there is laid up for me a crown of righteousness, which the Lord, the righteous judge, will give me at that day" (2 Timothy 4:7, 8).

Paul assures confidently.

The very nature of the covenant of grace and of God's declared purposes in the appointment and character of that covenant plainly shows that it is God's design to give ample provision to the saints of an assured hope of eternal life while they live here on earth. "The covenant is ordered in all things and sure." God's promises are explicit, often repeated and demonstrated in various ways. There are many witnesses to them and many seals of them. God has confirmed His promises with an oath. It is God's declared design in all of this that the heirs of the promises might have an undoubting hope and full joy in the assurance of their future glory (see Hebrews 6:17, 18).

Such confidence is based on God's confidence.

Yet such confidence cannot be taken for granted.

Moreover, it appears that assurance is not just attainable in some very extraordinary cases, but that *all* Christians are instructed to give all diligence to make their calling and election sure, and so they are told how they may do it (2 Peter 1:5-8). Indeed it is spoken of as very unbecoming to Christians not to know whether Christ be in them or not. "Know you not your own selves, how that Jesus Christ is in you, except you be reprobates" (2 Corinthians 13:5; see also 1 John 2:3, 5; 3:14, 19, 24; 4:13; 5:2, 19).

It follows from what we have just said that it is very unreasonable to say that people are hypocrites and that their affections are wrong just because they do not doubt their salvation and because the affections that they are subject to have banished all fears of hell.

Yet confidence as such is not enough.

On the other hand, their affections are not necessarily true just because they have boundless confidence that they are all right and that their affections are divinely inspired.[9] Nothing certain can be argued from their confidence, however great and strong it appears to be. Just because a man fearlessly calls God his Father, and prays often in the most intimate, bold, and appropriate language, it does not necessarily follow that his confidence rings true.

Indeed, such an overbearing, highhanded, and violent sort of confidence as this may not be evidence of true Christian assurance. For this may savor more of the spirit of the Pharisees who never doubted that they were saints. Indeed, they felt they were the most eminent of saints and were therefore bold to go to God and come near to Him and lift up their eyes and thank Him for the great distinc-

---

[9] "O professor, look carefully to your foundation: Be not high minded but fear." "You have it, it may be done and suffered many times in and for religion; you have excellent gifts and sweet comforts; a warm zeal for God and high confidence of your integrity: all this may be right, for aught that I, or it may be that you know; but yet it is possible it may be false. You have sometimes judged yourselves, and pronounced yourselves upright; but remember your final sentence is not yet pronounced by your Judge . . . your heart may be false, and you may not know it: Yea, it may be false, and you strongly are confident of its integrity" (Flavel, *Touchstone of Sincerity*, chapter 2, section 5).

tion He had given them before men. When Christ intimated that they were blind and graceless, they despised the suggestion: "And some of the Pharisees which were with Him heard these words, and said to Him, are we blind also?" (John 9:40). If they had had more of the spirit of the publican, they would have humbly trusted and hoped in Christ, having no confidence in themselves.

We only need to consider what is in the hearts of natural men, to realize how much they are under the dominance of self-exaltation and self-confidence. Once a hypocrite is rooted in such a false hope, he does not have the resources within himself to call his hope into question. In contrast, the true saint may doubt. There are four reasons for this.

For self-confidence is hypocrisy

First of all, the hypocrite does not have that cautious spirit, that great sense of the vast importance of a sure foundation, nor the dread of being deceived. The comforts of true saints will increase caution and a lively sense of how great and awful it must be to appear before the infinitely holy, just, and omniscient Judge. False comforts put an end to those things and dreadfully stupefy the mind.

Self-confidence has no real foundation.

Second, the hypocrite has no knowledge of his own blindness, nor of the deceitfulness of his heart, nor the mean opinion of his own understanding such as the true saint has. Those that are deluded with false discoveries and affections are always highly conceited of their own light and understanding.

Self-confidence is blind.

Third, the devil does not assault the hope of the hypocrite, as he does the hope of a true Christian. The devil is a great enemy to the true Christian hope, not only because hope tends greatly to comfort, but also because hope is of a holy, heavenly nature. It greatly tends to promote and to cherish grace in the heart; it is a great incentive to strictness and diligence in the Christian life. But the devil is no enemy to the hope of the hypocrite, which above all things establishes his self-interest.

Self-confidence is never challenged by the devil.

Self-confidence has a false hope.

Fourth, he who has a false hope is not aware of his own corruptions. A saint is. A true Christian is ten times more aware of his heart and his corruptions than is a hypocrite. Therefore his sins and practice will look dreadful to him. But it is false hope that hides corruption, covering it up so that the hypocrite looks clean and bright in his own eyes.

Two kinds of hypocrite

But there are two sorts of hypocrites. The first is deceived with his outward morality and external religion. The second is deceived with false discoveries and elevations of spirit. Such often talks of free grace but at the same time makes a righteousness of discoveries and of experience of humiliation, exalting to heaven with them. Thomas Shephard, in his exposition of *The Parable of the Ten Virgins*, distinguishes these two kinds of hypocrites by calling them *legal* and *evangelical* hypocrites. He often speaks of the latter as the worse, for it is evident that the latter is far more confident in his hope and the least likely to be dissuaded about it. I have scarcely known an instance of such a one in my life who has not been deceived.

The confidence of many of the *evangelical* hypocrites is like the confidence of some madmen who think they are kings and maintain this against all reason and evidence. So in one sense this is much more immovable than a truly gracious assurance. In contrast, a true assurance is not upheld dogmatically but only by a devout disposition where grace is maintained deeply within the soul. It is when the actions of grace decay in a Christian's life that he falls into a lifeless state, and loses his assurance. But the kind of confidence that hypocrites have will never be shaken by sin. This is sure evidence of their delusion.[10]

---

[10]Thomas Shepard speaks of it as "a presumptuous peace that is not interrupted and broken by evil works" (*Parable of the Ten Virgins*, part I, p. 139). Dr. Ames speaks of it as a thing by which the peace of a wicked man may be distinguished from the peace of a godly man, "the peace of a wicked man continues, whether he performs the duties of piety and righteousness or not; provided those crimes are avoided that appear to be horrid to nature itself" (*Cases of Conscience*, book 3, chapter 7).

Here I cannot but observe that there are certain doc- **False doctrines of**
trines often preached to people that should be given more **the self-confident**
caution and explanation because they tend to establish
the delusion and false confidence of hypocrites. I speak of
the doctrines of those who "are Christians living by faith,
not by sight; giving glory to God by trusting Him in the
dark; living upon Christ, and not upon experience; not
making their good dispositions the foundation of their
faith." These are excellent and important doctrines when
they are rightly understood, but when misunderstood they
can corrupt and be destructive.

The Scripture speaks of living or walking by faith and
not by sight with respect to eternal realities. These
realities are still unfulfilled and unseen. So it is clearly evident to anyone who looks at Scripture that faith is set in
opposition to sight (2 Corinthians 4:18; Hebrews 11:1, 8,
13, 17, 27, 29; Romans 8:24; John 20:29). However,
many falsely interpret this to mean that Christians ought
firmly to believe they should trust in Christ without
spiritual sight or light, even though they are in a dead and
dark frame of mind, and have no spiritual experiences or
insights. But to confidently assert that we ought to believe
and trust without spiritual light or sight is antiscriptural
and an absurd doctrine. The Scripture is ignorant of any
faith in Christ that is not founded in a spiritual sight of
Christ. To believe on Christ is to "see the Son and believe
on Him" (John 6:40). So faith that is without spiritual
light is not the faith of the children of the light and of the
day; rather, it is the presumption of the children of darkness.

It is the duty of God's people to trust in Him when in **God's people may**
darkness. They may remain still in the darkness in that **have to walk in**
they have to trust in God when the aspects of His provi- **darkness.**
dence are unseen. It may look as though God has forsaken
them and does not hear their prayers. Many clouds may
gather and many enemies may surround them formidably,
threatening to swallow them up. All events of providence

seem to be against them and all circumstances seem to render the promises of God too difficult to be fulfilled. Yet God must be trusted when He is out of sight, when we cannot see how it is possible for Him to fulfill His Word.

When everything but God's Word makes it look so unlikely, it is then that people must believe with hope against hope. Thus the ancient patriarchs, Job, the Psalmist, Jeremiah, Daniel, Shadrach, Meshech, Abednego, and the Apostle Paul gave glory to God by trusting Him in the darkness. We have many instances of such glorious faith in the eleventh chapter of Hebrews. But how different a thing this is than a trust in God that lacks spiritual sight and a mindset that is dead and carnal!

God's people may experience being destitute.

It is also possible that spiritual light be let into the soul in one way but not in another. Saints can trust in God, assured of their well-being even while they are destitute of some kinds of experience. For example, they may have clear views concerning God's efficiency and faithfulness, and so confidently trust in Him, knowing that they are His children. At other times, they may not have those clear and sweet impressions of His love. Thus it was with Christ Himself in His last passion. They may see the reality of God's sovereignty, holiness, and all-sufficiency, which enables them to submit quietly to Him and to exercise a sweet and encouraging hope in God's fulness even when they are not satisfied with their own good estate. Yet how different these things are from confidently trusting in God without spiritual light or experience!

Faith in itself means nothing.

Those who insist, therefore, that people live by faith when they have no experience and are in a poor spiritual condition have absurd notions of faith. He, they argue, who maintains his hope of his spiritual condition confidently and immovably while having little light or experience or while in the worst and most depressed state of mind, is the best man and honors God the most. They feel this evidences that he is strong in faith, having hoped against all hope, and thus is giving glory to God. But what Bible is it that says that faith is a man's confident believing that he is in such a good estate?[11] If this is faith, the Pharisees then had it *par excellence.* Scripture represents faith as that by which men are brought into a good estate; therefore it cannot be the same thing as believing that they are already there in that condition. Doubtless vast mischief has been done by these teachings.

XII. OUTWARD EVIDENCES ARE NOT ENOUGH TO DEMONSTRATE TRUE RELIGIOUS AFFECTIONS

True saints do not have the discernment to determine who are the godly and who are not. For although they may know experientially what true religion is in the internal exercises of it, they cannot feel or see into the heart of another person.[12] They can only see outward appearances. But the Scripture plainly intimates that this way of judging by outward appearances is at best uncertain and is liable to deceive. "The LORD sees not as man sees; for man looks on the outward appearance, but the LORD looks on the heart" (1 Samuel 16:7). "He shall not judge after the sight of his eyes, neither reprove after the hearing of his ears" (Isaiah 11:3).[13] Those who are quick to determine other people's condition are commonly poor judges and dangerous counselors. They betray one of three

---

[11]"Men do not know that they are godly by simply believing that they are godly. We know many things by faith." "By faith we understand that the worlds were made by the word of God" (Hebrews 11:3). Faith is the evidence of things not seen (Hebrews 11:1). "But it is not this way that godly men do know that they have grace. It is not revealed in the word, and the Spirit of God does not testify to particular questions" (Stoddard, *Nature of Saving Conversion,* pp. 83, 84).

[12]"Men may have the knowledge of their own conversion: the knowledge that other men have of it is uncertain, because no man can look into the heart of another and see the workings of grace there" (Stoddard, *Nature of Saving Conversion,* chapter 15).

[13]Mr. Stoddard observes, "all visible signs are common to converted and unconverted man; and the relation of experiences among the rest" (*Appeal to the Learned,* p. 75). Edwards also quotes Flavel at length: "Oh, how hard it is for the eye of man to discern betwixt chaff and wheat! And how many upright hearts are now censured, whom God will clear! How many false hearts are now approved whom God will condemn! Men ordinarily have no convincing proofs, but only probable symptoms; which at most beget but a conjectural knowledge of another's state" (*Husbandry Spiritualized,* chapter 12).

things: that they have had little experience; that they have poor judgment; or that they have an exaggerated amount of pride and self-confidence which distorts their perception of themselves. Wise and experienced men will proceed with great caution in such matters.

Outward show is not enough.

When the appearances seem to them exceedingly attractive, even the best of men may be deceived and their love won. It has been a common thing in the Church of God for such appealing professors to be received as eminent saints, and then later to fall away and come to nothing.[14] We need not be surprised about this if we consider the things that have already been observed, for we have shown that men may have religious affections of many kinds and yet not have a spark of grace in their hearts. So they may have a pseudoaffection toward God that closely resembles real love of Him. They may appear to the brethren as having a great admiration of God's affections and works, as demonstrating sorrow for sin, and as showing reverence, submission, self-abasement, gratitude, joy, religious longings, and zeal for religion and the good of souls. Their pseudoaffections may come after great revivals and conviction of conscience, and there may be great appearances of a work of humiliation.

Knowledge of the Bible is not enough.

These so-called saints may be able to quote many verses containing precious promises that have made a great impression upon them. They may pray and ardently glorify God, fervently calling upon others to praise Him, and crying out about their unworthiness and extolling the free grace of God. These actions may suggest their life as saints, and yet there may be nothing in them of the influence of the Spirit of God. Instead, they are the illusions of

---

[14]"Be not offended, if you see great cedars fall, stars fall from heaven, great professors die and decay: do not think they be all such: do not think that the elect shall fall. . . . The Lord who delights to manifest that openly, which has hid secretly, sends a sword in the fall" (Shepard, *Parable of the Ten Virgins*, part 1, pp. 118, 119). "The saints may approve thee and God condemn thee. You have a name that you live and are dead" (Revelation 3:1). (Flavel, *Touchstone of Sincerity*, chapter 2, section 5).

Satan and of a wicked and deceitful heart. But what indecent self-exultation and arrogance it is when poor, fallible, and ignorant mortals pretend that they can determine and know who are really sincere and upright before God and who are not!

Many emphasize the importance of evidences and use them to discern another's real piety, especially when the person's story harmonizes with their own experience and so touches their hearts. But these things are not certain and they cannot be depended upon because a true saint greatly delights in holiness; this is the most beautiful thing in His eyes. But whether these pleasing appearances are genuine or not is another matter.

Having proofs is not enough.

It is strange how people are never content with the rules and directions that Christ has given to them. Instead they go and invent ones that seem wiser and better. But I know of no directions or counsels which Christ ever delivered more plainly than the rules He has given to guide us in our judgment of people's sincerity. He says we should judge the tree chiefly by the fruit.

Yet there are many times when we cannot know a person's true state. Only God can.

Arrogant, then, is the notion of some who imagine that they know the godliness of others. The great Apostle Peter could only say that he *supposed* Sylvanus to be a faithful brother (1 Peter 5:12) even though Sylvanus appears to have been a very distinguished servant of Christ, an evangelist, a famous light in God's church during that time, and also an intimate companion of the apostles! (See 2 Corinthians 1:19; 1 Thessalonians 1:1; 2 Thessalonians 1:1).

Part III
THE DISTINGUISHING SIGNS OF TRULY GRACIOUS AND HOLY AFFECTIONS

III
HOW TRULY GRACIOUS
AFFECTIONS ARE KNOWN

efore we examine the distinguishing characteristics of true affections let me make three observations.

We cannot confi-
dently tell who
are real
Christians.

In the first place, I want to emphasize that I am in no
way trying to give sufficient evidence how we may distinguish true affection from false. It would be arrogant of me
to do so. For although it is clear that Christ has given rules
to all Christians in order to enable them to judge those
who merely profess to be saved and to keep them from falling into the snare set by false teachers, yet it is also clear
that it was never God's purpose to give us any set rules by
which we may confidently know the distinction between
sheep and goats. On the contrary, it is God's purpose to
reserve this for Himself, as His prerogative. So we can
never anticipate having clear evidences in this world. All
that we can expect are those that Christ has given us in
the Word of God, or that we can gather from it.

We can never
know how defec-
tive we can
afford to be as
Christians.

Second, Christians who are living in a low state of
grace or have fallen away from God into a dead and
worldly condition can never expect to have such signs. It
is not agreeable to God's purpose that they should know
their true condition. Nor is it desirable that they should.
We have every reason to thank God that He has made no

provision for us to know how sinful we can be. Indeed, there is a twofold deficiency which makes it impossible for the Christian who is in a low state of grace to know with certainty that he has real grace. For it is his very lack of grace which makes it difficult for him to discern clearly and certainly. When Christians are in a poor condition, guilt lies on the conscience, and this brings fear and so prevents the peace and joy of an assured hope.

There is also a defect of vision. The lack of grace and the dominance of sin weaken the vision so that one's visual perceptions are inaccurate. Similar to the plight of the person who is color blind, the person who is in a worldly condition is not able to judge spiritual realities properly.

For these reasons no evidence can be given to satisfy people in such a low spiritual condition. Even if the evidences were infallible and distinctive, they still would not serve them. But it is like a man given a rule about how to distinguish visible objects in the dark. Everything may be distinctly and clearly described to him, yet he just cannot see because he is in the dark. Too many people in this condition will spend many fruitless hours poring over past experiences, introspectively examining themselves according to what they have heard from the pulpit or have read in books. All their self-examination is futile. Their sin and worldly condition, like Achan's, must be slain, and until this is done they will continue to be in trouble.

It is thus God's purpose that man should obtain assurance in no other way than by the mortification of what is corrupt and by increasing in grace and the exercising of it. Although self-examination may be of great help and importance, and by no means should be neglected, it is not the principal way by which saints can be assured of their true condition. Assurance is not to be obtained as much by *self-examination* as it is by *action.* The Apostle Paul sought assurance in this way by "forgetting the things that were behind, and reaching forth unto those things that were before, pressing towards the mark for the prize of the high calling of God in Christ Jesus; if by any means he might obtain unto the resurrection of the dead" (Philippians 3:11, 13). And so it was chiefly in this way that he obtained assurance, saying, "I therefore so run, not as uncertainly" (1 Corinthians 9:26). He obtained assurance of winning the prize more by running than by considering. The swiftness of his pace did more to give him the assurance of victory than did the strictness of his examination.

Likewise the Apostle Peter exhorts us to give all diligence to growing in grace by adding to faith, virtue, and so on for "making our calling and election sure and for having an entrance into Christ's everlasting kingdom ministered to us abundantly" (2 Peter 1:5-11).

Good rules may help to distinguish true grace from what is counterfeit, but still I do not pretend to lay down any such rules as being sufficient in themselves.

Third, there is not much hope that those who practice false affections are likely ever to be rebuked by rules. They are so settled in false confidence and in the conceit of their own supposed experiences and privileges that they are blind and hardened in their own self-righteousness. Usually this is so secretive and subtle that it appears under the guise of great humility and they appear invincible to any such exposure. Of course their state is deplorable, and next to those who have committed the unpardonable sin. Some of these hypocrites seem to be out of reach of any conviction and repentance.

Rules will never restrain the self-confident.

Nevertheless, to lay down good rules may be a means of preventing such hypocrites and convicting others. For God is able to convict even these; His grace is not limited in any way. Moreover, such rules may help real Christians detect what are false affections, which they may have mingled with true. Rules may help their faith become purer, like gold tried in the fire.

With this introduction I now proceed directly to enumerate those twelve ways in which true religious affections are to be distinguished from false.

I. TRUE SPIRITUAL AFFECTIONS ARE
DIVINELY GIVEN*

True saints who are sanctified by the spirit of God are called spiritual persons in the New Testament. Their spirituality is distinctive and it distinguishes them from those who are not sanctified. The Apostle contrasts those who are spiritual with those who are natural and carnal. "The natural man receives not the things of the Spirit of God; for they are foolishness unto him; neither can he know them, because they are spiritually discerned. But he that is spiritual judges all things" (1 Corinthians 2:14, 15). This Scripture means that an ungodly man who has no grace is simply a natural man. The Apostle Jude speaks of certain ungodly men who had crept in unawares among the saints, "who are devoid of the Spirit" (Jude 4, 19). The Apostle explains they behave like this because they are *sensual.* This is the same word that is used in 1 Corinthians chapter 2 where it is translated *natural.* So he sums it up, saying, "And I, brethren, could not speak unto you as unto spiritual, but as unto carnal," or unsanctified. That the Apostle Paul means *unsanctified* by *carnal* is abundantly evident in other passages, such as Romans 7:25; 8:1, 4-9, 12, 13; Galatians 5:16; and Colossians 2:18.

Just as the saints are called spiritual in Scripture, so also are certain qualities and principles associated with them. We read of "a spiritual mind" (Romans 8:6, 7) and of "spiritual wisdom" (Colossians 1:9), and of "spiritual blessings" (Ephesians 1:3).

What it means to
be spiritual

The term *spiritual* in these and other texts in the New Testament does not refer to the soul or spirit as distinct from the body or the material part. Qualities are not spiritual because they have their seat in the soul and not in the body. These may be carnal or fleshly. This is true of pride and self-righteousness and of a man who trusts in his

---

*Jonathan Edwards wrote about the twelve signs of religious affections. This Roman numeral and the ones that follow consecutively in this book indicate his numbering of those signs.

own wisdom; these the Apostle calls *fleshly* (Colossians 2:18). Some things are not called spiritual because they are immaterial. The wisdom of the wise men and of the princes of this world is conversant with spirits and immaterial things. Yet the Apostle still speaks of these men as natural, totally ignorant of those things that are truly spiritual (1 Corinthians 2:6-8).

In the New Testament, persons or things are termed spiritual in relation to the Spirit of God. "Spirit" is the word that is used to signify the third person in the Trinity. It is therefore substantive of what the Scriptures mean by spiritual. Thus Christians are called spiritual persons because they are born of the Spirit and because of the indwelling and holy influences of the Spirit of God in them. Things that are called spiritual are related to the Spirit of God Himself. "Which things also we speak, not in the words which man's wisdom teaches, but which the Holy Ghost teaches; comparing spiritual things with spiritual. But the natural man receives not the things of the Spirit of God" (1 Corinthians 2:13, 14). Here the Apostle himself expressly signifies that by spiritual things he means the things of the Spirit of God, and those things which the Holy Spirit teaches (cf. Romans 8:6, 9).

Thus, it is only in relationship to the Spirit of God and His influences that persons and things are called spiritual. Moreover, it is not those who have had on occasion some common influence of the Holy Spirit who are spiritual. By spiritual it is meant those who are habitually godly men, as opposed to those men who are carnal and unsanctified. Clearly the Apostle means by spiritually minded those who are graciously minded (Romans 8:6). Some may have extraordinary gifts of the Spirit, yet not be spiritual persons as the New Testament understands the term (see Galatians 6:1). Natural men might have those same gifts.

It is evident from many scriptures that natural man may be subject to many influences of the Spirit of God (Numbers 24:2; 1 Samuel 10:10; 11:6; 16:14; 1 Corinthians 13:1-3; Hebrews 6:5, 6, and many others). Yet those people are not in the sense of the Scripture spiritual

Only the Holy Spirit makes us to be spiritual.

persons. Nor are any of the effects, common gifts, qualities, or affections that are from the influence of the Spirit
of God upon them called spiritual things. A great difference lies between these two things.

The Holy Spirit dwells in His people.

In the first place the Spirit of God is given to dwell
within the true saint as His proper, permanent abode. It is
His purpose to influence their hearts as the principle of a
new nature, or as a divine supernatural spring of life in action. The Scriptures represent the Holy Spirit not only as
moving and occasionally influencing the saints, but also
as dwelling in them as His temple, His proper abode, and
everlasting dwelling place (1 Corinthians 3:16; 2 Corinthians 6:16; John 14:17). He is represented as being so
united to the facilities of the soul that He becomes a principle or spring of new nature and life.

The Holy Spirit is their source of life.

Therefore the saints are said to live by Christ living in
them (Galatians 2:20). Christ by His Spirit not only *is* in
them but *lives* in them. They live by His life. His Spirit is
united with them as the essence of life in them. They not
only drink living water but this "living water becomes a
well or fountain of water" within the soul "springing up
into spiritual and everlasting life" (John 4:14), and thus it
becomes a principle of life in them. The Evangelist himself explains living water to mean the Spirit of God (John
7:38, 39). The light of the Son of Righteousness does not
only shine upon them but it is so communicated to them
that they shine also and become little images of that Son.
The sap of the true vine is not just conveyed into them as
the sap of a tree may be tapped off into a vessel, but it is
conveyed as sap is from a tree into one of its living
branches where it becomes the very substance of life. The
Spirit of God is so communicated and united to the saints
that forever afterward they are truly called spiritual.

On the other hand, although the Spirit of God may influence natural man in many ways, He is not communicated to them as an indwelling principle. They are unable
to derive any character from Him because there is no
union and so He is not their own.

A second reason why the saints and their virtues are called spiritual is that the Spirit of God, dwelling as a vital principle in their souls, will produce those effects which express His own nature. Holiness is the character of the Spirit of God and therefore He is called in Scripture the Holy Spirit. Holiness, which is the beauty and sweetness of the divine nature, is the proper nature of the Holy Spirit as much as heat is the property of fire, or sweetness is the property of holy anointing oil, as it was symbolized in the Mosaic Dispensation.

The Holy Spirit acts in holiness in them.

The Spirit of God dwells in the hearts of the saints as a seed, or spring of life, that exerts and communicates His own sweet and divine nature. The soul is made a partaker of God's beauty and Christ's joy so that the saint has true fellowship with the Father and His Son, Jesus Christ. This communion is the participation of the Holy Spirit. The grace which is in the hearts of the saints is of the same nature as the divine holiness. It is the same nature as the brightness of the sun but it cannot compare with the sun in its fulness. Therefore Christ says, "That which is born of the Spirit, is spirit" (John 3:6). But it is infinitely less in degree. It is like the brightness that is in a diamond which the sun shines on.

The Holy Spirit links them in fellowship with God.

But the Spirit of God never influences the minds of natural man in this way. Although He may influence them in many ways, He never, in any of His influences, communicates Himself to them according to His own proper nature. Indeed, when the Spirit of God moved upon the face of the waters (Genesis 1:2) there was nothing of the proper nature of the Holy Spirit in the motion of the waters. Similarly, He may act upon the minds of men in many ways without communicating Himself.

Thus the character and way in which the Holy Spirit operates in the saints is vastly different from anything man naturally knows or experiences. Not only are the people who have the Spirit of God dwelling in them called spiritual, but so also are their affections and distinctive

The Holy Spirit gives His people spiritual affections.

experiences. These differ totally from anything natural to man. It is a work that is peculiar to the Spirit of God.

This truth is expressed in Scripture by such phrases as "the saints being made partakers of a divine nature" (2 Peter 1:4), and "having God dwelling in them, and they in God" (1 John 4:12, 15, 16; 3:24). It is "having Christ in them" (John 17:21; Romans 8:10). It is "being the temples of the living God" (2 Corinthians 6:16). It is "living by Christ's life" (Galatians 2:20). It is "being made partakers of God's holiness" (Hebrews 12:10). It is "having Christ's love dwelling in them" (John 17:26). It is "having His joy fulfilled in them" (John 17:13). It is "seeing light in God's light, and being made to drink of the river of God's pleasures" (Psalm 36:8, 9). It is "having fellowship with God," or communicating or partaking with Him (1 John 1:3).

This does not mean, however, that the saints are made partakers of the essence of God, and so are deified with God, or "christified" with Christ, as is erroneously and falsely taught by some. But it does mean, to use the biblical phrase, that they are made partakers of God's fulness (Ephesians 3:17-19; John 1:16), that is, partakers of God's spiritual beauty and happiness according to the measure and capacity of a creature. This is what the word "fulness" signifies in biblical language. This is what I mean, then, by those influences that are divine when I say that truly gracious affections arise from those influences that are spiritual and divine.

Only God's people are therefore truly spiritual. True saints have only that which is spiritual; others have nothing which is divine in the sense that we have spoken of. They do not have the communications of the Spirit of God to the same degree as the saints; in fact, they have nothing of that nature or kind at all. The Apostle James tells us that natural men have not the Spirit. Christ teaches the necessity of a new birth, or being born of the Spirit, since man is only naturally born of the flesh and has no spirit (John 3:6). The Apostle Paul teaches that all who have the Spirit of God dwelling in them are His (Romans 8:9-11). Having the Spirit of God is spoken of as a pledge for an eternal inheritance, "the earnest" of it (2 Corinthians 1:22; 5:5; Ephesians 1:14). "Hereby know we that we dwell in Him, because He has given us of His Spirit" (1 John 4:13).

But the natural man has not experienced anything that is spiritual. He is not a "partaker of God's holiness" (Hebrews 12:10). "The natural man receives not the things of the Spirit of God; for they are foolishness to him: neither can he know them, because they are spiritually discerned" (1 Corinthians 2:14). Christ teaches us that the world is wholly unacquainted with the Spirit of God, "even the Spirit of truth, whom the world cannot receive, because it sees Him not, neither knows Him" (John 14:17). Christ likewise reproves the Pharisees, because they "had not the love of God in them" (John 5:42). Hence, natural men have no communion or fellowship with Christ, no participation with Him. Natural men are represented in Scripture as having no spiritual light, no spiritual life, no spiritual being.

These Scriptures show that the gracious influences to which the saints are subject and the effects of God's Spirit which they experience are entirely beyond nature or natural qualifications. They are not just different in degree, they are different in kind. This is what I mean by saying that they are supernatural, and therefore the gracious affections are those which come from supernatural influences.

God's gracious influences are divinely given.

The result is a new kind of inward perception which sanctifies the mind. It is a new way of perceiving, of thinking, and of consciousness. It is operated by grace as an entirely new kind of principle. Hence the work of the Spirit of God in regeneration is often compared in Scripture to the giving of a new sense: giving eyes to see, ears to hear, and turning darkness into light. It is compared with being raised from the dead to a new creation.

This new spiritual sense and its new dispositions are not just new facilities, they are new principles of life. A new foundation is laid for the very nature of the soul.

Being spiritual is having a wholly new life.

God's assistance to natural man is not spiritual.

The Spirit of God in all His operations upon the minds of natural man only moves, impresses, assists, improves, or in some way acts upon natural principles. He gives no new spiritual principle. Thus when the Spirit of God gives a natural man visions, as He did Balaam, He only impresses a natural principle, such as the sense of sight. But He gives no new sense. There is nothing supernatural, spiritual, or divine about it. So if the Spirit of God impresses a man's imagination either in a dream or when he is awake, He is only the stimulation of ideas similar to the kind he had by natural principles and senses. Thus the Spirit of God by His common influences may assist man's natural ingenuity, as He assisted Bezaleel and Aholiab in the skilled works of the tabernacle. He may assist man's natural abilities and political affairs and improve their courage, as when He put His Spirit on the seventy elders, and upon Saul to give him another heart. Conscience, too, may be aroused in this way.

Being spiritual is the possession of a whole new life.

But the spiritual influences of the Spirit of God on the hearts of His saints operate by infusing or exercising new, divine, and supernatural principles. These are principles which are of a new and spiritual nature, vastly nobler and more excellent than all that is in natural man.

At the same time there are two things needed to modify this statement.

Yet the spiritual life does share some things in common with the natural life.

First, not everything belonging to the spiritual affections is new and entirely different from what natural man conceives and experiences. Some things true of these gracious spiritual affections are true of other affections. Thus the saint's love of God is similar to a man's natural love of another person. Love of God makes a man desire to honor God and to please Him. A natural man's love for his friend makes him desire to honor and please him. Yet the saint's knowledge of the loveliness of God and his delight in Him are distinctive. The desire is not the same. It is like two people who have different tastes. One has acquired the sweet taste of honey but the other has never tasted honey. Therefore their tastes will be quite different.

Second, a natural man may have religious apprehensions and affections which are new and surprising to him and which he had never conceived of before. Yet these are not to be compared with the radically new principle of affection that the Holy Spirit brings to a man. Throughout this discourse I have insisted upon this matter, namely that all truly gracious affections only arise from the special and peculiar influences of the Holy Spirit. Again I emphasize that the natural imagination a person may have of God or of heavenly things, which does not come by the Spirit of God, is quite different from what we have described. This is true even though such imaginations can sometimes raise the natural affections of man to great heights of eloquence and wonder. Even the remembrance of words of Scripture when they are communicated only to the natural mind and imagination does not have the same reality. So Balaam might know that the words which God suggested to him were indeed suggested to him by God, and yet have no vital spiritual knowledge.

The natural man may also experience new things.

One may ask, "Is it possible for us to have any particular spiritual application of the promises of Scripture by the Spirit of God?" I answer that there is doubtless such a thing as a spiritual and saving application of the invitations and promises of Scripture to the souls of men. But it is also certain that the nature of it is wholly misunderstood by many people to the great ensnaring of their souls, giving Satan a great advantage over them and against the interest of true religion and of the Church of God. The spiritual application of a Scripture promise does not consist in its being immediately suggested to the thoughts by some external agent. It is a spiritual application of all of the Word of God, and of applying it to the heart in spiritually enlightening, sanctifying influences.[1]

How then can we apply God's Word spiritually to our lives?

---

[1]Thomas Shepard in *Sound Believer* says "embrace in your bosom not only a few promises but all. . . . When he takes all the Scripture and embraces it as spoken to him, he may then take any particular promise boldly. . . . This no hypocrite can do; this the saints shall do, and by this they may know when the Lord speaks in particular to them" (p. 159).

It is by having a relish for God's promises.

A spiritual application of an invitation or offer of the gospel consists in giving the soul a spiritual sense or relish of the holy and divine blessings offered, and the sweet and wonderful grace of the offerer in making so gracious an offer. It also relishes in the holy excellence of the Promiser and His faithfulness to fulfill what He offers, and in His glorious sufficiency. The heart is then led and drawn forth to embrace the offer. This gives the person evidence of title to the thing offered. Hearts, too, are drawn forth to embrace the Promiser as well as the thing promised. Thus they are enabled to see their grace and their title to the promise.

His Word does not speak magically.

We are not talking about some sudden revelation of secret facts by immediate suggestion or somehow being spiritual and divine. This is not the way gracious effects and operations come. For example, if it is suddenly revealed to me that next year this country will be invaded by a fleet from France, or that such and such persons will then be converted, or that I myself shall then be converted, this has nothing of the nature of the spiritual and divine operation.

To think that the Holy Spirit of God acts in this way with His dear children is a mean and shameful notion. It greatly debases the high and exalted kind of influence and operation of the true witness of the Spirit.[2]

The Holy Spirit is not auto-suggestion.

The idea of *witness* has misled many in their notion of this kind of influence of the Spirit of God. By this they mean an inward immediate suggestion, as though God inwardly spoke to the man and testified directly to him, and told him that he was His child by a kind of secret voice or impression. They do not realize that although the word *witness* or *testimony* is often used in the New Testament, it

---

[2]Jonathan Edwards's father-in-law, Solomon Stoddard, "In his youth, fell in with the opinion of others about this notion of the Spirit coming by immediate suggestion. But in the later part of his life, when he had more thoroughly considered matters and had more experience, he entirely rejected it as is evidenced by his treatise on *The Nature of Saving Conversion* (p. 84).

is not in this sense. For it is not the mere declaring and asserting a thing to be true that proves its truth, but the demonstration of evidence. Thus in Hebrews 2:4, God is said to "bear witness, with signs and wonders, and divers miracles, and gifts of the Holy Ghost." Now these miracles He has spoken of are called God's witness, not because they are the nature of assertions, but because they are evidences and proofs (cf. Acts 14:3; John 5:36).

When the Scripture speaks of the seal of the Spirit, it is an expression which properly denotes not an immediate voice or suggestion, but some work or effect of the Spirit that is left as a divine mark upon the soul as evidence of how God's children might be known. When God sets His seal upon a man's heart by His Spirit, there is some holy stamp, some image impressed and left upon the heart by the Spirit, just as a seal makes an imprint upon the wax. This is what the Scripture means by the seal of the Spirit. This image is imprinted by the Spirit on the hearts of God's children; it is His own image. In ancient times seals were engraved with two things: the image and the name of the person whose seal it was. So the seal of the Spirit indicates both His likeness and also His possessions.

The seal of the Spirit is His likeness upon us.

Another proof that the seal of the Spirit is no magical revelation of any fact by immediate suggestion, but instead is grace itself in the soul, is that the seal of the Spirit is called the earnest of the Spirit in our hearts (2 Corinthians 1:22; cf. Ephesians 1:13-14) in Scripture. Now the earnest is a part of a promised inheritance that one day will be fully possessed. This earnest of eternal life is grace. Our inheritance in Christ is not any extraordinary gifts, but it is His vital indwelling in our hearts, communicating Himself there, His own holy and divine nature. This is what is intimated in Galatians 3:13, 14.

The earnest of the Spirit is the gift of His nature to us.

Hence the Spirit is often spoken of as the sum of all the blessings promised in the gospel (Luke 24:49; Acts 1:4; 2:38, 39; Galatians 3:14; Ephesians 1:13). This inheritance is the great legacy which Christ left His disciples and the Church in His last will and testament (John 14, 15,

16). This is the sum of the blessings of eternal life which shall be given in heaven. (Compare John 7:37-39; John 4:14; Revelation 21:6; 22:1, 17). This vital indwelling of the Spirit in the saints is then "the earnest of the Spirit, the earnest of the future inheritance, and the first fruits of the Spirit"[3] as the Apostle calls it (Romans 8:22).

In adopting us the Holy Spirit gives us the nature of Christ in His sonship. In Romans 8:14-16 the Apostle plainly speaks of the Spirit giving us witness or evidence that we are God's children because He dwells in us. He gives us a spirit of adoption so we might be disposed to behave toward God as to a Father. And what is this spirit, but the spirit of love? The Apostle distinguishes between two kinds of spirits: the spirit of a slave, that is a spirit of fear; and the spirit of a child or the spirit of adoption, that is love. The Apostle says that we have not received the spirit of slaves which is a spirit of fear, but we have received the noble spirit of children, a spirit of love, which naturally disposes us to go to God as children to a father, and behave toward God as children. This is the evidence or witness which the Spirit of God gives us that we are His children.

The new child within us is His Spirit. I am convinced therefore that the Apostle has a special regard for the spirit of grace as a spirit of love, that is the spirit of the child in its dynamic activity. For it is only perfect love, or strong love, which can witness and evidence that we are children, when it casts out fear and wholly delivers us from the spirit of bondage. It is this spirit of childlike, evangelical, humble love to God that gives clear evidence of the soul's relation to God as His child. Hence the child within us can cry out, "Abba, Father."

The Apostle said that "the Spirit bears witness with our spirits." By our spirits is meant our conscience, which is also called the spirit of man. For "the spirit of man is a candle of the LORD, searching all the inward parts" (Proverbs 20:27). We also read of the witness of this spirit of ours: "For our rejoicing is this, the testimony of our con-

---

[3]Shepard, *Parable of the Ten Virgins*, part 1, p. 86.

science" (2 Corinthians 1:12; cf. 1 John 3:19-21). When the Apostle Paul speaks of the Spirit of God bearing witness with our spirit, he is not to be understood as having two spirits that are separate, collateral, and independent witnesses. It is by one that we receive the witness of the other. So the Spirit of God gives this evidence by infusing and shedding abroad the love of God, as the spirit of a child, in our hearts.

Many mischiefs have arisen from the false and delusive notion of the witness of the Spirit that say it is a kind of inward voice, or suggestion, or declaration of God to man that he is beloved of Him, and pardoned, elected, etc. This is affirmed with, and sometimes without, the text of Scripture. Many false, vain, yet excited affections have arisen from this. It is to be feared that multitudes of souls have been eternally undone by it. That is why I have spent time on this topic. But now I proceed to a second characteristic of gracious affections.

IV
THE OBJECT AND FOUNDATION
OF GRACIOUS AFFECTIONS

he fundamental object of gracious affections is the glory of God, so in no way can these affections be conceived to bear any relation to self or to self-interest.

II. THE FUNDAMENTAL BASIS OF GRACIOUS AFFECTIONS IS THE TRANSCENDENT EXCELLENCE AND LOVEABLE NATURE OF DIVINE THINGS.

By this, I do not mean to exclude all relationships that bear on divine things. Clearly they may have a secondary and consequential influence on those affections that are truly holy and spiritual, as I shall show later.

As I have already observed, the affection of *love* is the fountain source of all affections. Christian love particularly is the spring of all gracious affections. Yet it is the divine excellency and glory of God in Jesus Christ, the Word of God, the works of God, and the ways of God that are the primary reason a true saint loves these things and not any supposed interest the believer has, or will receive from them, or any imagined relation which they bear to his interest. Self-love can never be said to be the underlying foundation of his love for the affections.

Self-love is never the true source of gracious affections.

Some argue that all love arises from self-love. They say it is impossible in the nature of things for any man to have any love for God or any other being except that self-love be the foundation of it all. May I humbly suggest that they have not reflected seriously enough about this. They argue that whoever loves God and desires His glory and the enjoyment of Him only does so for his own sake. The glory of God and the enjoyment of His perfections, they argue, are merely things which are agreeable to man and which tend to make him feel good. He is really placing his happiness in these feelings and desires. So they say it is from self-love or a desire for his own well-being that any man desires God to be glorified.

Why give glory to God?

But they should reflect further and inquire how is it that man first came to place his happiness in God's glorification and in the contemplation and enjoyment of God's perfections. There is no doubt that man does place his happiness in these things. Why, then, did they become so important that he esteems it his highest lesson to glorify God? Is this not the fruit of love? For a man must first love God and be one with Him in heart before he will esteem God's good as his own.

It is not strong arguing to say that after a man has his heart united to God in love, he desires God's enjoyment and glory, and therefore it was that desire that was the creator of his love. It cannot be argued that because a father begat a son, that therefore the son begat the father. Is this not still self-love, a love for his own well-being even in his desire to glorify and enjoy God? Is there not then some prior principle even before self-love that motivates someone to apprehend intrinsically the beauty, glory, and supreme good in God's nature? Might it not be this that first draws a man's heart to God and causes his heart to be united to Him, prior to all considerations of his own interest or happiness?

There is nothing divine about self-love.

There is of course the kind of love or affection that a person has toward other people or things which clearly comes from self-love. It is based upon a preconceived relationship the person feels or demands of the other. But when the first thing that draws someone's attraction to another is seeing those qualities and virtues that are recognized as lovely in themselves, love will develop very differently from love that arises from self-interest. It is different from the self-love that arises from some gift bestowed by another, as a judge loves and favors a man who has bribed him.

This kind of affection for God or Jesus Christ which arises from self-love cannot be truly a gracious and spiritual love. Love for God in self-interest cannot be confused with true love for God that comes from precious affections. For self-love is common to both men and devils. There is nothing divine about that.[1] As Jesus asked: "If you love them that love you, what thanks have you? For sinners also love those that love them" (Luke 6:32). Love which arises from self-interest is worthless in the sight of God. It reminds us of Satan's challenge of Job's integrity: "Does Job serve God for nothing? Have not You made a hedge about him, and about his house?" (Job 1:9, 10). God would not have allowed this objection to be raised if the accusation had not had some basis.

It is a reasonable affirmation then that the basis of a true love for God is His intrinsic worth, for He is worthy to be loved for His own sake. It is this which makes Him so worthy of love. His divine excellence is so glorious. This is why God is God: to be loved for His own sake.

God must be loved for His own sake.

Some people who never see the glory and beauty of God in Christ may be motivated by self-love for God. But gratitude may be merely natural, just as anger is. Anger arises when self-love is crossed. Gratitude is an affection one has because another loved him or benefited him in some way. Both are expressions of self-love. For there can

---

[1]"There is a natural love to Christ, as to one that does you good and for your own ends; and there is spiritual love for Himself whereby the Lord alone is exalted" (Shepard, *Parable of the Ten Virgins*, part 1, p. 25).

be a form of gratitude which does not come from any true or proper love. Christ speaks of this type of gratitude in Luke 6:32 where He says that sinners love those who love them. Likewise, Saul was greatly affected by gratitude to David for sparing his life, yet he remained a habitual enemy of him. We have many examples of this kind of gratitude in Scripture.

Self-love may express itself in gratitude. Gratitude is a natural principle of human nature and thus renders ingratitude so much more vile and heinous. Someone who suppresses gratitude is described as having such a high degree of wickedness that they are without natural affection (Romans 1:31). If the lack of gratitude or natural affection is evidence of great sin, this is still no argument that all gratitude and natural affection have the nature of saving grace.

Self-love, expressed in mere natural gratitude, may be a spring that issues in some kind of love for God. Such love may come from a false notion of God that people have been taught which says God is only goodness and mercy and will never exercise justice. Or perhaps that God's goodness depends upon what they themselves define to be good. On false grounds such as these, men may love a god of their own imagination and be far removed from loving the true God who reigns in heaven.

Self-love may have no sense of sin. Again, self-love may originate an affection in men toward God that is quite ignorant of their real condition before Him. Lacking a conviction of conscience, they are unaware of the heinousness of their sin against God. They have formed in their own minds a god that suits them, and they think of God as merely one like themselves, who favors and agrees with them, and loves just like them. They have no idea how far away they are from loving the true God.

Again, others develop a high affection for God as a result of their fears of hellfire which are followed by some assuring text of Scripture that persuades them they are safe and that God has forgiven them and made them His children. But their perspective is distorted, and because of their selfish pride they may even continue to have false notions of their communion with God, believing it is carried on by impulses and whispers and other external manifestations that really come from their own imagination.

The exercises of true and holy love in the saints come in a very different way. It is not primarily that they first see that God loves them and therefore He is to be loved, but rather that they first see that God Himself is lovely. Christ appears so glorious and excellent that their hearts are enraptured by Him alone. This then is what really motivates their true love of God.[2] The affection of the saints begins with God Himself. Self-love is then only of secondary consequence. In contrast, false affections begin with self and an acknowledgment of the excellence of God is only dependent and consequent upon the primary attitude of self-interest. But God is the ultimate foundation in the love of the true saint. Everything else is built upon this foundation.

However, self-interest may influence people corporately as well as privately. For example, in time of war a nation will view its successes or defeats in this way. So self-interest can be extended cosmically to all the works of mankind.

But I do not want to imply from what I have said that all gratitude to God is merely natural, or that there is no such thing as spiritual gratitude as a holy and divine affection. I have simply illustrated that there is an affection which is the exercise of natural gratitude. But of course there is such a thing as gracious or true gratitude which greatly differs from what natural men experience. It differs in two ways.

First, true gratitude or thankfulness to God for His kindness to us arises from a love for God, based on who He is in Himself. Natural gratitude has no such basis. The gracious stirrings of natural affections to God for kindness

True gratitude is for what God is in Himself.

---

[2]"There is a sight of Christ which a man has after he believes, namely that Christ loves him. But I speak of a prior vision of Him that precedes the second act of faith. This is an intuitive or real sight of Him as He is in His glory" (Shepard, *Parable of the Ten Virgins*, part 1, p. 74).

received always spring from the primary love already in the heart, which is for God's own excellence.

Because of the love that already exists, the affections are disposed to flow out on occasions of God's kindness. Since he has seen the glory of God, and since his heart is already overcome by it and is captivated with love to Him on that account, the saint's heart is tender and easily affected by subsequent kindnesses he receives. It is like a man's gratitude to a dear friend who is loved and held in high esteem by him. Due to his view of his friend, the man's heart is all the more sensitive and tender toward him and therefore more easily affected with gratitude. Thus self-love is not excluded from a gracious gratitude. The saints do indeed love God for His kindness to them. "I love the Lord, because He has heard the voice of my supplication" (Psalm 116:1). But something else is included, for another love has already prepared the way and laid the foundation for these grateful affections.

True gratitude is for what God has done in Christ.

Second, in gracious gratitude, men are affected with the attributes of God's goodness and free grace, not only as these attributes affect their own interest, but as they relate to the glory and beauty of God's nature. The wonderful and unparalleled grace of God is manifested in the work of redemption, and shines forth in the face of Jesus Christ as being infinitely glorious in itself. So the saint who exercises a gracious thankfulness for it sees it to be what it is in itself, and delights in it as such. God's personal kindness to them is like a magnifying glass that God sets before them in order to behold the detail of the beauty of the attribute of God's goodness. In holy thankfulness to God, the saint's concern enables him to focus more sharply upon God's goodness. But the source of his thankfulness is in the excellence of God Himself.

Some may perhaps be ready to object against this argument and quote: "We love Him because He first loved us" (1 John 4:19), as if this implied that God's love to the true saints was the first cause of their love for Him.

In answer to this, I would note that the Apostle's purpose is to magnify the love of God to us by showing that

He loved us when we had no love for Him. (See verses 9, 10, and 11). He shows that God's love to the elect is the ground of their love to Him in three ways.

First, the saints' love to God is the fruit of God's love to them; it is the gift of that love. God gives them a spirit of love for Him because He loved them from eternity. His love is the foundation of their regeneration and the whole of their redemption.

Our love to God is God's gift to us.

Second, the work of redemption that God has made by Jesus Christ is one of the chief ways in which God has revealed the glory of His moral perfection to both angels and men. It is the major basis of the reality that God is love.

Our love to God is evidence of His redemption.

Third, God's love to one whom He has chosen, which the person discovers by his own conversion, is a great evidence of God's moral perfection and glory to him personally. This then is a real stimulus to have the love of holy gratitude to God. So the statement that the saints love God because He first loved them fully answers the purpose of the Apostle's argument in this text. In no way can this verse be used to contradict the principle that a spiritual and gracious love in the saints arises essentially from the excellence of God in Himself.

Our love to God is evidence of God's choice of us.

As it is with the love of the saints, the primary basis of their joy, spiritual delight, and pleasure is not any consideration of their own interest in divine things. Again, primarily, it consists in the sweet contemplation of the beauty of divine things in themselves. So it is also in contrast to the joy of the pseudo-Christian who is self-congratulatory, with self as the basis for joy. Whereas the true Christian rejoices in God, for true saints have their minds delighted only with the realities of God and of His things.

The basis for the true delight that a real Christian has is in God and in His perfection. His delight is in Christ, and in His beauty. God appears as He is in Himself, the chief among ten thousand and altogether lovely. The saint sees

The true Christian delights only in God Himself.

that the holy doctrines of the gospel are upheld in recognizing that God is to be exalted and man to be abased. The saints rejoice in God and that Christ is theirs. They first rejoice in the excellence and glory of God Himself and only in a secondary way rejoice that so glorious a God is theirs. However, the hypocrites have a joy that is only a joy in themselves and not in God.

The false Christian delights in his own experiences.

When false believers congratulate only themselves, they keep their eyes only upon themselves. Having received what they call spiritual discoveries or experiences, their minds are taken up with self and the admiration of their experiences. What they are chiefly excited about is not the glory of God or the beauty of Christ but the thrill of their own experiences. They keep thinking, "What a wonderful experience this is! What a great discovery that is! What wonderful things I have encountered!" And so they put their experiences in the place of Christ and His beauty and all-sufficiency. Instead of rejoicing in Christ Jesus, they indulge in their own wonderful experiences. They are so caught up in their own imagination about these great and wonderful experiences, that all their notion of God relates merely to them. As their emotions intensify, these hypocrites will sometimes be completely swallowed up in narcissism, self-conceit, and a fierce zeal with what is happening. But it is all built like a castle in the air that has no foundation other than imagination, self-love, and pride.

True Christians talk much about God.

As are the thoughts of this kind of person, so is their talk. They are great talkers about themselves. In contrast the true saint, under great spiritual affections and from the fulness of his heart, is ready to speak much about God, His glorious perfections and works, the beauty and winsomeness of Christ, as well as the glorious things of the gospel. So a true saint is so wrapped up in the enjoyment of the true discoveries of the sweet glory of God and Christ that he never sees himself and his own attainments. These would only be a diversion and loss which he could not bear to have; he never wants to take his eye off the ravishing object of God.

As the love and joy of false Christians are from self-love, so are their other affections. Their sorrow for sin, their humiliation and submission, their religious desires and zeal are all related to self-love and its lusts. It is easy for nature, corrupt as it is, under the notion of already having a god who protects and favors them in their sins, to love this imaginary god that suits them so well, and to extol him, submit to him, and to be zealous for him. They assume they are eminent saints, so if their self-opinion were to collapse, so would their affections. This would happen if they had even a glimpse of their true sinfulness. Since their affections are built upon self, self-knowledge would destroy them.

All the affections of the self-loving are false.

But truly gracious affections are built elsewhere. They have their foundation not in self, but in God and Jesus Christ. Therefore a discovery of themselves and of their own sinfulness will purify their affections; it will not destroy them. In some ways it will sweeten and heighten them.

Only those who love God can afford to love themselves.

III. Gracious Affections Are Based on the Delight of the Beauty and Moral Excellence of God Himself

Or, to put it in another way, a love of divine things because of the beauty and sweetness of their moral excellence is the beginning and source of all holy affections.

For those who do not understand what I mean, let me explain. The word *moral* is not to be understood here in the popular sense of morality or moral behavior as meaning outward conformity to duties. I do not mean simply virtues such as honesty, justice, generosity, good nature, and public spirit as referring to external attitudes in

What is moral excellence?

opposition to those virtues that are more inward, spiritual, and divine, such as holy faith, love, humility, and heavenly-mindedness of true Christians. I repeat, the word *moral* is not to be understood in this way.

To understand rightly what I mean, it must be observed that theologians commonly make a distinction between moral good and evil, and natural good and evil. By moral evil is meant the evil of sin or what is contrary to that which is right. By natural evil is meant things such as the evil of suffering, pain, torment, disgrace, etc. These things are contrary to the ideal state of what is good and bad.

Likewise theologians make a distinction between the natural and moral perfections of God. By the moral perfections of God they mean those attributes which God exercises as a moral agent: His righteousness, truth, faithfulness, and goodness; or in a word, His holiness. By God's natural attributes or perfections they mean those attributes, according to our way of conceiving God, that consist of His greatness, His power, His knowledge, His eternal being, His omnipresence, and His awful and terrible majesty.

Holiness is moral excellence.

The moral excellence of an intelligent, free being is located in the heart or will of moral agents. Therefore the intelligent being, whose will is truly right and lovely, is morally good and excellent.

The moral excellence of an intelligent being, when it is true and real and not merely external or counterfeit, is holiness. Therefore holiness comprehends all the true moral excellence of intelligent beings. It is the only true virtue. Holiness comprehends all the true virtues of a good man such as his love to God, his gracious love to men, his justice, his charity, his mercy, his gracious meekness and gentleness, and all the other true Christian virtues that he has. Holiness in man is but the image of God's holiness.

God's two-fold image in man.

Just as there are two kinds of attributes of God according to our way of conceiving Him in terms of His moral attributes as summed up in holiness and in terms of His natural attributes of strength, knowledge, etc. that constitute His greatness, so there is a two-fold image of God in man. There is His moral or spiritual image, which is His holiness which man forfeited by the fall, and there is God's natural image which is man's reason and understanding, his natural ability, and dominion over creatures.

Now you can understand what I mean by saying that a love for divine things, for the beauty of their moral excellence, is the beginning and spring of all holy affections. We have already noted that the first objective basis for all holy affections is the supreme excellence of divine things as they are in themselves, according to their own nature. Now let me proceed further, and say more specifically that the first objective ground of all holy affections is their moral excellence or holiness. Holy persons in the exercise of holy affections love divine things primarily because of their holiness. They love God in the first place because the beauty of His holiness or His moral perfection is supremely lovable in itself. Not that the saints love God only for His holiness. All His attributes are attractive and glorious to them. They delight in every divine perfection. But their love of God for His holiness is what is most fundamental and essential in their love. It is here that true love of God begins. All other holy love for divine things flows from this.

All gracious affections are based upon a love of God's holiness.

The true beauty and loveliness of all intelligent beings essentially consists in their moral excellence or holiness. This is true of God, according to our way of seeing Him: holiness is in a unique manner the beauty of the divine nature. Often we read of "the beauty of holiness" (Psalm 29:2; 96:9; 110:3). It is this that renders all His other attributes glorious and lovely. It is the glory of God's wisdom that it is a holy wisdom and not wickedly subtle or crafty. It is this that makes His majesty lovely and not terrible and dreadful. It is a holy majesty. It is the glory of God's immutability that it is a holy immutability and not an inflexible obstinacy in wickedness.

The vision of God's beauty is the source of true affections.

The sight of God's loveliness must begin here. A true love of God must commence with a delight in His holiness and not with a delight in any other attribute. No other attribute is truly lovely without it. So if the true loveliness of all God's perfections arises from the loveliness of His holiness, then the true love of all His perfections arises from the love of His holiness. Those that do not see the glory of God's holiness cannot see anything of the true glory of His mercy and grace. They see nothing of the glory of those attributes in themselves.

The beauty of saints is their holiness.

As the beauty of the divine nature primarily consists in God's holiness, so does the beauty of all divine things. Herein consists the beauty of saints, that they are saints or holy ones. The moral image of God in them is their beauty and their holiness. The beauty and brightness of the angels of heaven is this: they are holy angels and not devils (Daniel 4:13, 17, 23; Matthew 25:31; Mark 8:38; Acts 10:22; Revelation 14:10). The Christian faith is beautiful above all other religions because it is so holy a religion. The excellence of the Word of God consists in its holiness. "Your word is very pure and therefore Your servant loves it" (Psalm 119:140, cf. 128, 138, 172; Psalm 19:7-10).

The beauty of the Lord Jesus is His holiness.

His holiness primarily creates the winsomeness and beauty of the Lord Jesus as a chief among ten thousands and altogether lovely. He is the Holy One of God (Acts 3:14; 4:27; Revelation 3:7). The spiritual beauty of His human nature consists in His meekness, loveliness, patience, heavenly-mindedness, love of God, love of men, condescension to the mean and unattractive, compassion to the outcast, etc. All are summed up in His holiness. All the beauty of His human nature consists primarily then in His holiness.

The glory of the gospel is its holiness.

Likewise the glory of the gospel is largely that it is a holy gospel, the bright expression of the holy beauty of God in Jesus Christ. Spiritual beauty arises from the holiness of its doctrine. The way of salvation is a holy way; this is beauty. The glory of heaven as the Holy City of Jerusalem is that it is the habitation of God's holiness and so of His glory (Isaiah 63:15). All the beauties of the new Jerusalem as described in the last two chapters of Revelation are various representations of this (Revelation 21:2, 10, 11, 18, 21, 27; 22:1, 3).

Because of this holy excellence, the saints love all these things. They love the Word of God because it is pure. They also love the saints. Likewise, heaven is lovely and those holy tabernacles of God are amiable in their eyes. So too, they love God and Jesus Christ and their hearts delight in the doctrines of the gospel and they sweetly walk in the way of salvation that is thus revealed.[3]

The love of the saints is for holiness.

Under the heading of the first distinguishing mark of gracious affections, I observed that a new spiritual sense is given to those that are regenerated. This is different from all the other five senses that we naturally have. This is nothing other than the beauty of holiness.

The Scripture often represents the beauty and sweetness of holiness as the great object of a spiritual taste and appetite. This was the sweet food of the holy soul of Jesus Christ. "I have meat to eat that you know not of . . . my meat is to do the will of Him that sent me, and to finish his work" (John 4:32, 34). Psalm 119 emphasizes and describes this appetite more than any other passage. In the first verses the Psalmist sets out to seek this. Throughout the Psalm the excellence of holiness is represented as the immediate object of a divine taste, relish, appetite, and delight in God's law.

The longing of the saints is for holiness.

A holy love has a holy object. The holiness of love consists chiefly in this, that it is the love of what is holy. Likewise a holy nature must need holy things, things

---

[3]"A right relationship with Christ's person is always required, in order to taste the bitterness of sin as the greatest evil. A man will never be close with Christ, unless he recognizes His holiness and sees that from Him is the greatest good. For we have told you that a right relationship with Christ comes only in recognizing His holiness" (Shepard, *Parable of the Ten Virgins*, part 1, p. 84).

which are consistent with itself. And so above all else the holy nature of God, Christ, the Word of God and other divine things must be consistent with the holiness of the saints.

Likewise what is sinful has enmity against God. So what is carnal is against holy things, against God, against the law of God, and also against the people of God. They have contrary natures. It is contrary to contrary and like to like. Wickedness hates holiness and holiness delights in holiness.

The eternal interest of heaven is on holiness.

In heaven attention is engaged perfectly upon the holiness of divine things. It is divine beauty that chiefly enraptures the admiration and praise of the bright and burning seraphim. "One cries unto another, and says, 'Holy, Holy, Holy is the Lord of Hosts, the whole earth is full of His glory'" (Isaiah 6:3). "They rest not day and night saying, 'Holy, Holy, Holy, Lord God Almighty, which was, and is, and is to come'" (Revelation 4:8). So the glorified saints also cry: "Who shall not fear Thee, O Lord, and glorify Your name? For You only are holy" (Revelation 15:4).

The test of the affections is their focus on God's holiness.

The Scriptures represent the saints on earth as adoring God primarily for His holiness. They admire and extol all His attributes, seeing the loveliness of His holiness. Thus when they praise God for His power, His holiness is the beauty which motivates them. "O sing unto the Lord a new song, for He has done marvelous things: His right hand and His holy arm has gotten Him the victory" (Psalm 98:1). Likewise they praise Him for His justice and awful majesty (Psalm 99:2, 3, 5, 8, 9). They praise God for His mercy and faithfulness. "Light is sown for the righteous, and gladness for the upright in heart. Rejoice in the Lord, you righteous; and give thanks at the remembrance of His holiness" (Psalm 97:11, 12). "There is none holy as the Lord: for there is none beside You; neither is there any rock like our God" (1 Samuel 2:2).

The test of affections, particularly love and joy, lies in whether or not holiness is the foundation of the affections. This is the difference between true saints and natural men. Natural men have no sense or taste of the goodness and excellence of holy things. It is wholly hidden from them. But the saints, by the mighty power of God, have discovered it. It captivates their hearts and delights them above all things. By this you may examine your love to God and to Jesus Christ and to His Word, and your joy in them, and your love also to the people of God, and your desires after heaven. This is the real test.

Natural men may see the great power and awful majesty of God. Circumstances force them to do so. It is said that when Christ comes "In the glory of His Father, every eye shall see Him." "Then they will cry to the mountains to fall upon them and to hide them from the face of Him that sits upon the throne" (Isaiah 2:10, 19, 21). God has often declared that it is His immutable purpose to make all His enemies know Him in this way, saying, "They shall know that I am the Lord." "As truly as I live, all the earth shall be filled with the glory of the Lord" (Numbers 14:21).

The saints, like natural men, will also see the greatness of God. But it will affect them differently. Instead of being terrified they will rejoice and praise God. They see the beauty of His holiness, not terror.

Natural men have no sense of God's holiness.

V

THE FORMATION OF GRACIOUS AFFECTIONS

oly affections do not have heat without light. Constantly there must be the information of the understanding, so that there is spiritual instruction which the mind receives as light or actual knowledge.

IV. GRACIOUS AFFECTIONS ARISE FROM A SPIRITUALLY ENLIGHTENED MIND

The child of God is graciously affected because he sees and understands something more of divine things than he did before. He sees more of God and Christ and of the glorious things which are revealed in the gospel. He has a clearer and better view. Either he will receive new understanding of divine things or his former knowledge will be renewed after the view has faded. "Everyone that loves, knows God" (1 John 4:7). "I pray that your love may abound more and more in knowledge, and in all judgment" (Philippians 1:9; cf. John 6:45; Colossians 3:10). Knowledge, then, is the key that first opens the hard heart, enlarges the affections, and so opens the way for men to enter the Kingdom of Heaven. "You have taken away the key of knowledge" (Luke 11:52) is then a serious charge.

Many false affections do not come from the understanding.

But there are many affections which do not arise from any light in the understanding. And when this happens, it is a sure evidence that these affections are not spiritual, however elevated they appear to be.[1] They may even have new apprehensions which they did not have before. But the nature of man is such that it is impossible for his mind to be affected unless he has apprehended or conceived of something. But many people are affected by apprehensions or conceptions which have nothing of the nature of knowledge or instruction in them. For example, someone may be suddenly struck with a bright idea and yet there is nothing of the nature of instruction about it. People never become the wiser by such things, or indeed have more knowledge about God or the way of salvation. For these external ideas have no acquaintance with God, nor do they communicate understanding of Him.

Gracious affections are enlightened by the mind.

True spiritual and gracious affections are not aroused in this way. They come from the enlightening of the mind in order to understand the things that are taught of God and Christ in a new way. This comes through a new understanding of the excellent nature of God, His wonderful perfections, or from some new view of Christ in His spiritual excellencies and fullness. These are entirely different in their character from any ideas or stimuli that come naturally to man.

Even those affections that come from reading texts of Scripture are futile unless specific instruction is received in the understanding from those texts. When Christ used the Scripture to make the heart burn with gracious affection, He did so by opening the Scriptures to people's understanding. "Did not our hearts burn within us, while He talked with us by the way, and while He opened to us the Scriptures?" (Luke 24:32). He gave explicit instruction to the minds of the disciples.

---

[1]Shepard, *Parable of the Ten Virgins*, part 1, p. 146.

False affections arise then from ignorance rather than from instruction. Even in impromptu prayer it is possible for some to be so affected by what they say that their affections are intensified. Or it may be that some apt thoughts come to their mind from the Scriptures and so they say the Spirit of God is teaching them. Through ignorance in these and other ways, people mistakenly think this is the Holy Ghost visiting them because their minds are stimulated and affected. At first this may bring great joy, but in the confusion of emotions that follow, they begin to be discouraged. Such stimuli do not produce true spiritual affections.

False affections come from ignorance.

But the Scriptures are able to give to the saints spiritual and supernatural understanding of divine things which is unknown to those who are not true Christians. It is this that the Apostle speaks of: "But the natural man receives not the things of the Spirit of God; for they are foolishness unto him; neither can he know them, because they are spiritually discerned" (1 Corinthians 2:14). It is a way of seeing and discerning spiritual things that is also spoken of: "Whosoever sins has not seen Him, neither knows Him" (1 John 3:6). "He that does evil has not seen God" (3 John 11; cf. John 6:40; 17:3).

This is demonstrated many times in the Bible. There is an understanding of divine things which in its nature and character is wholly different from all knowledge that natural men have. The Scripture calls this spiritual understanding. "We do not cease to pray for you, and to desire that you may be filled with the knowledge of His will, in all wisdom and spiritual understanding" (Colossians 1:9).

What then is this spiritual perception or apprehension that natural men do not have? I have already shown that this new spiritual sense which the saints are given is recognizing the supreme beauty and excellence of divine things as they are in themselves. The Scripture is in accord with this. The Apostle teaches very plainly that the great thing discovered by spiritual light and understood by spiritual

Spiritual understanding rests upon the holiness of God.

knowledge is the glory of divine things. "But if our gospel be hid, it is hid to them that are lost; in whom the god of this world has blinded the minds of them that believe not, lest the light of the glorious gospel of Christ, who is the image of God, should shine unto them" (2 Corinthians 4:3, 4). To this we add verse 6: "For God, who commanded the light to shine out of darkness, has shined into our hearts, to give the light of the knowledge of the glory of God in the face of Jesus Christ" (cf. 2 Corinthians 3:18).

And so we come to the conclusion that spiritual understanding consists in: "A sense of the heart for the supreme beauty and sweetness of the holiness of moral perfection of divine things, as well as all the discernment and knowledge of things of religion that depends on and flows from such a sense."

A sense of heart for divine things

Spiritual understanding consists primarily then in a sense of heart of spiritual beauty. I say a sense of heart, for it is not merely speculated. Nor can there be a clear distinction made between the two faculties of understanding and will as acting distinctly and separately. But when the mind is aware of the sweet beauty and amiableness of something, this sensitivity of its loveliness and delightful character gives one a taste, or inclination, or will for it.

Distinction must therefore be made between the mere notional understanding of a speculative mind, and the sense of the heart where the mind is not speculative but experiences and feels. It is the experiential knowledge which actually sees what is attractive or repulsive. The one is mere theory, the other is experienced knowledge, and the heart is its proper subject. The Apostle Paul speaks of mere speculative knowledge, "which has the form of knowledge and of the truth in law" (Romans 2:20). In contrast he speaks of the experienced taste when he says: "Now thanks be to God, which always causes us to triumph in Christ Jesus, and makes manifest the savor of his knowledge in every place" (2 Corinthians 2:14; cf. Matthew 16:23; 1 Peter 2:2, 3; 1 John 2:20).

Spiritual understanding primarily consists in the experiences or taste of the moral beauty of divine things. No knowledge except what arises from this sense can be called spiritual. Secondarily it includes all that discerns and experiences these divine things.

When the true beauty and attraction of the holiness found in divine things is discovered by the soul, a new world of perspectives is opened. The glory of all the perfections of God and of everything that pertains to Him is revealed. It shows the glory of all God's works both in creation and in providence. His works express the special glory of His holiness in His righteousness, faithfulness, and goodness. The glorifying of God's moral perfections is a special end of all creation. A sense of the moral beauty of divine things enables us to understand the sufficiency of Christ as Mediator. In this way the believer is led into the knowledge of the excellency of Christ's person. The saints are then made aware of the preciousness of Christ's blood and of its sufficiency to atone for sin. On this depends the merit of His obedience, and sufficiency and prevalence of Christ's intercession. The beauty of the way of salvation by Christ is made manifest in all these ways.

> The beauty of God gives us new vision.

Likewise there is seen the excellency of the Word of God. Take away all the moral beauty and sweetness of the Word and the Bible is left as a dead letter, dry, lifeless, and tasteless. So in all these ways, we learn to see no longer after the flesh: "For he has become a new creature; old things are passed away, behold all things are become new" (2 Corinthians 5:16, 17). Thus all true experienced religion comes from this sense of spiritual beauty. For whoever does not see the beauty of holiness cannot appreciate the graces of God's Spirit. Without this there is ignorance of the whole spiritual world.

Thus it is plainly obvious that when God implants the spiritual supernatural sense a great change is made in the heart of man. First, at conversion comes the first dawning

> The beauty of God brings conversion.

of a glorious light upon the soul. When sight is received by one who has been blind and with only four other senses, it is like seeing in the clear light of the sun and discovering a whole new world of visible objects. Yet this spiritual sense which we have spoken of is much nobler than that of any sense a man may naturally have. For the object of this sense is infinitely greater and more important.

The beauty of God tests all affections.

From this knowledge of divine things, all true gracious affections proceed. By this knowledge all affections are tested. Those affections that arise from any other kind of knowledge or from any other kind of apprehension are vain.

Without the beauty of God men's consciences are darkened.

To deepen the contrast between the experience of natural man and the saving knowledge of God's Spirit, we may cite the matter of conscience. When natural men are aroused to a sense of conscience, the Spirit of God gives them no knowledge of the true moral beauty which is in divine things. All that they have is a clearer sense of guilt, its punishment, and its connection with the evil of suffering. It is this that will fully awaken the consciences of wicked men without any spiritual light at the Day of Judgment. To a lesser degree it is the same with those who are awakened now in conscience, but who have no spiritual light in this world. In spite of their deeper apprehension of the character of sin and of evil, they are still left without any real understanding of the glory of God.

It is the beauty of God—not mere knowledge—that enlightens the mind.

From what has been said of the nature of spiritual understanding, it appears also that this does not consist in any new doctrinal knowledge nor in suggesting to the mind any new propositions or any further reading. For it is an experience and a new relish of beauty and sweetness. [2] So spiritual knowledge does not consist of any new doctri-

---

[2]Calvin in his *Institutes* says, "It is not the office of the Spirit that is promised to us, to make new and unheard of revelations, or to coin some new kind of doctrine which tends to draw us away from the received doctrine of the Gospel. For it is to seal and confirm to us in that very doctrine which is by the Gospel" (book 1, chapter 9, no. 1).

nal explanation of some Scripture. Doctrinal knowledge is only the explanation of some part of Scripture, given us to understand what are the propositions contained and taught in the context of Scripture. Thus the spiritual understanding of the Scripture does not consist merely in opening the mind up to the mystical meaning of the Scripture, its parables, types, and allegories. It is possible that a man might know how to interpret all of these things and have no saving grace. "And though I have the gift of prophecy, and understand all mysteries, and all knowledge, and have not charity, it profits me nothing" (1 Corinthians 13:2).

Again, spiritual knowledge is not merely people being informed about their duties. Knowledge of such duties would only be one aspect of doctrinal knowledge. A proposition concerning the will of God is properly a doctrine of religion as is a proposition that concerns the nature of God or the work of God. This is vastly different from spiritual knowledge. Balaam had immediate knowledge of the will of God suggested to him by the Spirit of God, from time to time, concerning the way that he should go, and what he should do and say. But there was no spiritual light in him.

Propositional knowledge is not enough.

So being led and directed in this way is not the holy and spiritual leading of the Spirit of God. This is only peculiar to the saints and is the distinguishing mark of the sons of God: "For as many as are led by the Spirit of God, they are the sons of God" (Romans 8:14).

Even if people suddenly have their actions directed and guided by some text of Scripture brought to them in some extraordinary fashion, the case is not altered. This does not necessarily make spiritual instruction. If, for example, someone is seeking guidance as to whether he should be a missionary in some heathen land and after earnest prayer he reads the instructions which God gave to Jacob: "Fear not to go down into Egypt; for I will go with you; and I will also surely bring you up again" (Genesis 46). This does not mean that God has promised to bring him back to New England again after his missionary travels. There is nothing of the nature of a spiritual or gracious leading of the Spirit in this, nor is there anything of spiritual understanding in it. Thus the understanding of a text of Scripture does not imply spiritual understanding.

How do we understand the Scriptures spiritually?

To spiritually understand the Scriptures rightly is to understand what is in the Scripture and to know its immediate intent. It is not the creation of a new meaning. When the mind is enlightened spiritually and rightly to understand the Scriptures, it is in order to see in the Scriptures what was not seen before because of blindness. So the Psalmist exclaims, "Open You my eyes, that I may behold wonderful things out of Your law" (Psalm 119:18). What is argued here is that the reason it was not seen the same as before was that the eyes were shut. But this is not to make a new meaning out of Scripture, as if one could make a new Scripture. This is adding to the Word, for which there is threatened a dreadful curse.

To understand the Scriptures spiritually is to have the eyes of the mind open, to behold the wonderful, spiritual excellence of the glorious things contained in its true meaning. This, ever since it was written, has always been contained in it. Such spiritual vision is able to see divine perfections, the excellence and sufficiency of Christ, and the way of salvation. It is able to see the spiritual glory of the precepts and the promises of Scripture which were always in the Bible, but were not seen before, but are now seen with a new meaning.

The gracious leading of the Spirit consists in two things. First, it is in instructing someone in his duty by the Spirit, and it is second in powerfully inducing him to comply with that instruction.

Having a spiritual sense

Such guidance is given by spiritual discernment and taste of that which has in it true moral beauty. This holy sensibility discerns and distinguishes between good and evil and between holy and unholy without the need of any logical reasoning. He who has a true relish of external beauty knows what is beautiful by looking at it. He needs no train of reasoning to do so. Whoever has a musical ear knows whether a sound is in true harmony; he does not need the reasonings of a mathematician to consider the proportion of the notes. Whoever has a taste for gourmet food does not need reasoning in order to know good food. "Does not the ear try words, and the mouth taste his meat?" (Job 12:11). Likewise, if an unworthy or unholy action is suggested to the spiritually discerning, a sanctified eye sees no beauty in it nor is pleased with it. Sanctified taste will only be nauseated by it. In this way a holy person is led by the Spirit by having a holy taste and disposition of heart.

Such a one judges what is right spontaneously without making any particular deductions or by having any arguments. Thus Christ blames the Pharisees that they "did not, even of their own selves, judge what was right" (Luke 12:57). The Apostle sees this clearly in judging spiritual beauty: "Be you transformed by the renewing of your mind, that you may prove what is that good, and perfect, and acceptable will of God" (Romans 12:2). There is therefore such a thing as having good taste for natural beauty. To have a sense of taste is to give things their real value and not to be dazzled with false lusters or be deceived in any way. Taste and judgment then are the same thing. And yet it is easy to discern a difference. The judgment forms its opinion from reflection whereas taste does not need this formality. Just as the ear can be upset with a harsh sound, or the sense of smell can be soothed by an agreeable perfume, so taste reacts immediately and anticipates all reflection. There is also spiritual taste which true Christians have to guide them and give them discernment by the Spirit of God.

Taste is judgment.

Where grace is strong and living, this holy disposition and spiritual taste will enable the soul to determine right and becoming actions. Real Christians know readily and exactly without further need of other abilities.

We see this illustrated in the way habits influence behavior. For example, if a man is very good natured, he will treat others with kindness. His good nature will influence him on each occasion to behave in speech and action in a way that is consistent with true goodness. Not even the strongest reason will help a man of a morose temper. Likewise, when a man's heart is influenced deeply by friendship and with strong affection for someone else, he will have a very different quality of kindness than someone who has all the capacities but not a disposition of heart. He has a spirit within him that motivates him. He senses habitual attitudes that prompt him to act spontaneously.

So spiritual disposition and godly taste teach and guide a man in his behavior in the world. An uneducated person who is deeply humble, meek, and has a loving disposition will be able to live according to Christian rules of humility, meekness, and charity far more readily and specifically than someone who does not have the disposition but studies diligently and reasons elaborately with a strong intellect. So too will a spirit of love to God in holy fear and reverence toward Him and with filial confidence in God and a heavenly-mindedness, teach and guide a man in his behavior.

But it is exceedingly difficult for an unrighteous man, who is destitute of Christian principles in his heart, to know how to behave like a Christian in all the life, beauty, and heavenly sweetness of such a holy and humble character. He does not know how to put on such garments, nor do they fit him. "The labor of the foolish wearies every one of them, because he knows not how to go to the city" (Ecclesiastes 10:15). But the "lips of the righteous know what is acceptable" (Proverbs 10:32). "The tongue of the wise uses knowledge aright: but the mouth of fools pours out foolishness" (Proverbs 15:2).

Spiritual taste is not always spelled out. In judging actions by spiritual taste, true saints do not have specific recourse to definite rules in God's Word with respect to every word and action that they have to communicate. Yet their taste itself is generally subject to the rule of God's Word and is tested and tried by it. Spiritual taste greatly helps a soul in reasoning upon the Word of God and in judging the true meaning of its rules. It removes the prejudices of a depraved appetite and leads the thoughts naturally in the right way.

It casts light on the Word of God and causes the true meaning most naturally to come to mind, because there is a harmony between the disposition and relish of a sanctified soul and the true meaning of the rules of God's Word. It is this harmony that also tends to bring to mind on proper occasions the very texts themselves. Thus the children of God are led by the Spirit of God, in judging actions themselves and in their meditating upon and applying the rules of God's Holy Word. Thus God teaches them His statutes and causes them to understand the way of His precepts. The Psalmist often prays for this.

It is in harmony with God's Word.

But this leading of the Spirit is very different from what some assume it to be. They think that God gives them new precepts by an immediate inner voice or suggestion. Yet this does not taste of the true excellence of things nor does it judge and discern rightly. They do not in fact learn what is the Word of God by such spiritual judgment, but rather see it as something to be done that is immediately dictated to them. In such cases there is no real judgment or wisdom. In contrast, the leading of the Spirit which is peculiar to God's children is imparted with that true wisdom and holy discretion which is so often referred to in the Word of God. This way is as contrasted as the stars above, and the glowworm below.

The leading of God's Spirit is not sensational but sensible.

True spiritual understanding is utterly different from all those kinds and forms of enthusiasm that imagine visions, inward suggestions, predictions of future events, immediate revelations of secret facts, etc. None of these composes a divine sense and relish of the heart or the holy beauty and excellence of divine things. Indeed, they have nothing to do with such a spirit. They are merely impressions in the head. These kinds of experiences and discoveries commonly excite the emotions and intensely delude people. But a very great part of false religion in the

Spiritual understanding is not just ecstatic.

world, from one age to another, consists of these types of experiences and delusions. Such were the experiences of the ancient Pythagoreans with their raptures, strange ecstasies, and pretense to divine contact and immediate revelations from heaven. Such also were the experiences of the Essenes, an ancient sect among the Jews, at and after the time of the apostles. Similar were the experiences of many of the ancient Gnostics, the Montanists, and other sects of ancient heresy in the early church.

True affections control the imagination.
But before I leave this subject, to prevent misunderstanding of what has been said, I would also like to note that I am far from saying that no affections are spiritual which are attended with imaginary ideas. Man's nature is such that he can scarcely think of anything intensely without some kind of outward ideas. When the mind is deeply engaged and the thoughts are intense, the imagination is often stronger and the outward idea is more alive, especially in people of a certain temperament. But there is a great difference between having lively imaginations arising from strong affections and strong affections arising from lively imaginations. The former, doubtless, may be often a case of truly gracious affections. Truly gracious affections do not arise from the imagination, nor do they have any dependence upon it. On the contrary, the imagination is only the accidental effect or the consequence of the affection through the infirmity of human nature. When the affection arises from and is based upon the imagination instead of having spiritual insight, the affection, however elevated it may be, is still worthless and vain.

Having observed this, I proceed to another mark of gracious affections.

VI
CERTAINTY AND HUMILITY IN GRACIOUS AFFECTIONS

V. GRACIOUS AFFECTIONS ARE ASSOCIATED WITH HISTORICAL EVIDENCE AND TRUE CONVICTION

his seems to be implied in the text which is the basis of this whole discourse: "Whom having not seen, you love; in whom, though now you see Him not, yet believing, you rejoice with joy unspeakable, and full of glory." All those who are truly gracious persons have a solid, full, fair, and effectual conviction of the truth of the great things of the gospel. By this I mean they no longer halt between two opinions. For them the great doctrines of the gospel have ceased to be doubtful or matters of mere opinion. Rather, they are matters which are settled and determined without a doubt.

So they are not afraid to venture everything upon their truth. Their conviction is an effective one. The great spiritual, mysterious, and invisible things of the gospel have reality and certainty. They have the weight and power of reality in their heart. Thus they rule their affections and control them for the rest of their lives. The reality of Christ as the Son of God and Savior of the world and the great things that He has revealed concerning Himself and His Father are no longer matters of speculation. They see the truth for what it is. Their eyes are opened so that

The reality of Christ is the basis of true affections.

117

they really see Jesus is the Christ, the Son of the living God.

They see revealed God's eternal purposes concerning fallen man and the glorious and everlasting things prepared for the saints in the world to come. These become matters of great weight with them. Having a mighty power upon their hearts, God's purposes influence their practice because they are viewed with infinite importance.

The truth of the gospel is the basis of gracious affections.

All true Christians have this conviction of the truth of the gospel. They see it abundantly revealed in the Holy Scriptures. I have only mentioned a few references. "'But whom say you that I am?' Simon Peter answered and said, 'You are the Christ, the Son of the living God.' And Jesus answered and said to him, 'Blessed are you, Simon Barjona; My Father, which is in heaven, has revealed it to you'" (Matthew 16:15-17; cf. John 17:6-8; 2 Corinthians 5:6-8; 2 Timothy 1:12; 1 John 4:13-16). "For whatsoever is born of God overcomes the world; and this is the victory that overcomes the world, even our faith. Who is he that overcomes the world, but he that believes that Jesus is the Son of God?" (1 John 5:4, 5). Therefore truly gracious affections are associated with a strong conviction and persuasion of the truth of the things of the gospel. The reality of this is clearly evidenced in these and other Scriptures.

But there are many other religious affections which are not associated with such a conviction. Many ideas and apprehensions which are affecting but not convincing may be called divine discoveries. They may persuade some for a time, but they have no permanent nor effective conviction. Some may even think that they have been converted by what they have become convinced of, yet they are not like those who live under the influence and power of a realizing conviction of the infinite and eternal things which the gospel reveals. If they were, it would be impossible for them to live as they do. For their affections are not associated with a thorough conviction of the mind upon which they entirely depend. It is like the crackling of thorns, or wisps of straw, or like a blade of grass on stony ground that has no root or depth of soil to maintain its life.

Some people, emotionally and self-confidently excited, speak ignorantly of seeing the truth of the Word of God. They are, in fact, very far away from it. Some text of Scripture comes to their mind in a sudden and extraordinary manner and they think it declares immediately to them that their sins are forgiven, or that God loves them, or that He will save them. In their excitement they call this "seeing the truth of the Word of God." But it is nothing but a delusion. To truly see the truth of the Word of God is to see the truth of the gospel, not a revelation that such and such persons shall go to heaven.

Suppose a person's belief in Christian doctrines does not simply come from his education, but is also supported by reasons and arguments. This still does not make his affections truly gracious ones. As we have seen, it is necessary that his beliefs should be not only reasonable, but that his affections should arise from true spiritual faith. I suppose no one will doubt that some natural men do reach out to the evidence of the truth of the Christian religion on the basis of rational proofs or arguments. Doubtless, Judas thought Jesus was the Messiah on the basis of the things which he saw and heard. Yet he was a devil all along. We read in John 2:23-25 that many believed in Christ's name when they saw the miracles that He did. Yet Christ did not trust them. Simon the sorcerer believed when he saw the miracles and signs which were done, yet he still remained bitter and in the bond of iniquity (Acts 8:13, 23). So too we may read of those who believed for awhile and were greatly affected, even joyfully receiving the word, yet their religious affections were not spiritual.

> **Rational proofs are inadequate for gracious affections.**

It is evident then that there is such a thing as a spiritual belief or conviction of the truth of the things of the gospel that is distinctive to those who are spiritual, regenerate, and have the Spirit of God dwelling in them as a vital principle. The conviction they have may not appear to differ from the seeming conviction of natural men because both are accompanied by good works, but the belief itself

> **Conviction is inadequate without experience of faith.**

is distinct. For natural men never have what is peculiar to those who are spiritual. This is evident by the Scripture. "They have believed that You did send Me" (John 17:8). "According to the faith of God's elect, and the acknowledging of the truth which is after godliness" (Titus 1:1). "The Father Himself loves you, because you have loved Me, and have believed that I came from God" (John 16:27). "Whoever shall confess that Jesus is the Son of God, God dwells in him, and he in God" (1 John 4:15, cf. 5:1).

What is spiritual conviction?

How then is one spiritually convicted? Conviction comes from the illumination of the understanding. A right judgment depends upon accurate comprehension. So too the spiritual conviction of the truth of the gospel arises from having a spiritual comprehension. Scripture often demonstrates that a saving faith is a saving belief that comes from the Spirit of God's enlightening the mind to view things correctly. It is as if things were unveiled or revealed to enable the mind to see them as they really are. "I thank You, O Father, Lord of heaven and earth, that You have hid these things from the wise and prudent and have revealed them unto babes: even so, Father, for so it seemed good in Your sight. All things are delivered unto me of my Father: and no man knows who the Son is but the Father; and who the Father is but the Son, and he to whom the Son will reveal Him" (Luke 10:21, 22; cf. John 6:40). This and other Scriptures indicate that true faith arises from a spiritual sight of Christ.

True conviction lies in spiritual understanding.

Scriptures in which Christ manifests God's name to the disciples are given for a true comprehension and view of divine things so that the disciples would know that Christ's doctrine "is of God, and that Christ Himself is of Him, and was sent by Him" (Matthew 16:16, 17; 1 John 5:10; Galatians 1:14-16).

This then is a spiritual conviction of the divinity and reality of what is revealed in the gospel, and it comes from a spiritual understanding of such things. Scripture is very plain and explicit about this. "If our gospel be hid, it is hid to them that are lost; whom the god of this world has blinded the minds of them that believe not, lest the light of the glorious gospel of Christ, who is the image of God, should shine upon them. For we preached not ourselves, but Christ Jesus the Lord; and ourselves your servants for Jesus' sake" (2 Corinthians 4:3-5). Nothing can be more evident than the saving belief of the gospel as spoken of here together with the last verse of the previous chapter, "but we all, with open face, beholding as in a glass the glory of the Lord, are changed into the same image, from glory to glory, even as by the Spirit of the Lord." This belief arises from the mind's enlightenment to behold the divine glory of the things it reveals.

Thus this view or sense of the divine glory and of the unparalleled beauty of the things exhibited to us in the gospel tends directly and indirectly to convince the mind of the gospel's divinity.

It is the vision of God that convinces.

First, there is the immediate conviction of the divinity of the things of the gospel because of the clear view given of their divine glory. This provides a reasonable conviction, since belief and assurance are both consistent with reason. For example, there is real evidence of the deity of Christ: God is revealed as God. He is distinguished from all other things and exalted above them all by His divine beauty which is infinitely different from all other beauty. The soul is thus given a kind of intuitive knowledge of the divinity of the things seen in the gospel. So it is not that a person judges the doctrines of the gospel to be from God without any criteria or deductions at all. He sees and recognizes divine glory.

It is a consistent vision.

It would be very strange indeed if any professing Christian were to deny the transcendence and absolute difference between the excellency in divine things and all other things. For instance, how vastly different is the speech of a learned scholar from that of a little child! How different again is their speech from that of some genius such as Homer, Cicero, Milton, Locke, or Addison! If then we

It is a unique vision.

122 The Distinguishing Signs of Holy Affections

cannot set limits on the degrees of mental excellence as
seen in speech, what of the perfections of God? Looking at
His perfections is like looking at the sun. In this way the
disciples were assured that Jesus was the Son of God, "for
they beheld His glory, glory as of the only begotten of the
Father, full of grace and truth" (John 1:14). When Christ
appeared in the glory of His transfiguration to His disiples,
His spiritual glory was made manifest to their minds. And
it was this that, with good reason, completely assured
them of His divinity. Later the Apostle Peter speaks of
this occasion: "For we have not followed cunningly de-
vised fables, when we made known unto you the power
and coming of our Lord Jesus Christ, but were eyewitnesses of His majesty. For he received from God the
Father, honor and glory, when there came such a voice to
Him from the excellent glory, 'This is my beloved Son, in
whom I am well pleased,' and this voice which came from
heaven we heard, when we were with Him in the holy
mount" (2 Peter 1:16-18).

It is a vision interpreted in the gospel.   Now this distinguishing glory of the divine Being has
its brightest appearance and manifestation in the gospel.
The doctrines that are taught there are spoken by the
Word and thus the divine council has been revealed.
These are the clearest, most distinguishing, and most attractive expressions of the glory of God's moral perfections ever made to the world. It is no argument to say that
not everyone sees the glory any more than it is to say
Milton is not a great author because not everyone appreciates him. Because men's sensibilities are corrupt,
men are hindered from seeing the reality of God in His
Word.

But a sense of the spiritual excellence and the beauty of
divine things tends to convince the mind of the truth of
the gospel. For as soon as the eyes are opened to behold its
beauties, the gospel is all seen immediately to be true.
Then a man sees how loathsome his sinfulness is. Tasting
the sweetness of true moral good, he also tastes the bitterness of moral evil. He sees the desperate depravity of his
own nature in a new way. The soul feels the pain of such a

loathsome disease, and he sees the corruption of original sin within him. He sees the need of a Savior, and of his need of the mighty power of God to renew his heart and to change his nature. In the Word he also begins to see the glory of the reality of God Himself.

In addition to all this, the Scripture shows that these things have to be experienced. For it is experience that convinces the soul; God knows the heart of man better than we can even know our own hearts, and He who perfectly knows the nature of virtue and holiness is the Author of the Scriptures. Now we begin to see with clarity the wonderful word and truth of the gospel, which was unknown before. It appears with a powerful and invincible influence on the soul. It persuades us indeed of the divine reality of the gospel.

It is a vision personally experienced.

A solid, reasonable persuasion and conviction of the truth of the gospel is more clearly seen by those who are literate and have a generally historical perspective of the truth of Christianity. Those who remain illiterate need to be convinced from point to point. But there will still be gaps where they ask, "How do I know this, or that?" Learned men will tell them about this or that, but questions still remain; so some continue with endless doubts and scruples.

But the gospel was not given only to the learned. There are at least nineteen in every twenty, or even ninety-nine in every hundred, for whom the Scriptures were written who are incapable of being convinced of the divine authority of the Scriptures by the arguments that a scholar may use. In His covenant of grace and in the manifold evidence of His faith, God has given His people a more general evidence of the truth of the gospel. As David says, "He made a covenant and an order in all things." His promises are sure. So we are exhorted: "Let us draw near, in full assurance of faith" (Hebrews 10:22; cf. Colossians 2:2).

It is reasonable to expect then that God would give the most explicit evidence of His faithfulness in the covenant of grace. It is wise and rational for us to desire most to have a full, unquestioning, and absolute assurance. But it is certain that such assurance will not be granted merely by arguments fetched up from ancient traditions or from histories and monuments.

Martyrs have died as witnesses to the truth.

If we read over the histories of the many thousands who died as martyrs for Christ since the beginning of the Reformation and who cheerfully underwent extreme tortures in the confidence of the truth of the gospel, we see how few of them were assured merely by arguments. Many of them were weak women and children, most were illiterate and only recently brought out of ignorance and darkness. They lived and died in a time when the arguments for the truth of Christianity had been very imperfectly handled.

But true martyrs of Jesus Christ are not merely those who strongly believe the gospel of Christ is true. They have seen the truth for themselves. The name of *martyr*, or *witness*, implies this. Witnesses of the truth are not those who simply declare an opinion that something is true. Proper witnesses are those who can and do testify that they have seen the truth of the thing that they assert. "We speak that we do know, and testify that we have seen" (John 3:11). Doubtless Peter, James, and John, after they had seen the excellent glory of Christ on the mount, would have been ready to speak as witnesses and to say positively Jesus is the Son of God. For as Peter says, "They were eyewitnesses" (2 Peter 1:16).

If experience is the first basis of evidence, the second basis is that a view of this divine glory convinces the mind more indirectly of the truth of Christianity. It does this in two ways.

A vision of God will remove prejudice.

First, it removes the prejudices of the heart against the truth of divine things. The mind is naturally full of enmity against the doctrines of the gospel. This is a disadvantage to arguments that seek to prove their truth and it causes them to lose their force upon the mind. But when a person has discovered the divine excellence of Christian doctrines personally, his enmity and prejudices are removed, sanctifying his reason and causing it to be opened freely. This removal of prejudice makes a vast difference in the force of an argument. Christ's miracles had a different effect on the disciples than they did on the Scribes and Pharisees, who were influenced by blinding prejudices that clouded their reason.

Second, divine glory not only removes rational hindrances, but it helps reason in a positive way by helping to focus the attention of the mind to have a clearer view of things and to see their mutual relationships. New light which impresses the mind with greater conviction is cast so that the mind can judge more effectively.

A vision of God convinces the mind.

In these ways we see that gracious affections are always associated with a strong conviction of their reality. But before I leave this topic, it is necessary to note some of the ways some may be deceived in this.

Some degree of conviction of the truth of these things comes from the common illuminations of the Spirit of God. Natural men may be convinced at times of revivals and be awakened to some degree of conviction of the truth of divine things. They may see evidences of God's greatness and majesty in His Word and works. This may make them sensible to the dreadfulness of His wrath for sin; therefore they may have a great dread and guilt. All this may tend to create religious convictions which yet have no spiritual conviction of their truth. So sometimes these are mistaken for saving convictions and their resulting affections.

Revival movements may lead to false convictions.

A second form of deception affects those with vivid imaginations. Sometimes they see visions and have locutions, all of which may bring a strong conviction of the truth of unseen things. But in the final analysis these tend to draw people away from the Word of God. It causes them to reject the gospel and to establish unbelief and atheism. Yet at first they may be persuaded that these things are revealed in the Scriptures. Then they discover that their confidence is founded on delusion and worth nothing. Such people, for example, may imagine that they saw Christ and heard Him speaking to them, and so they are confident there is a Christ. Or in Catholic churches they may be persuaded that a miracle has been

Intense imagination may also mislead.

wrought by Christ Himself. They may imagine that they saw Him weep or shed fresh blood, or even utter certain words. And so they are confident that there is indeed a Christ. But when they are convinced that perhaps they were deluded after all, they reject it all, truth as well as fiction. Even the intercourse which Satan has with witches, and their frequent experience of his immediate power has a tendency to convince them of the truth of some of the doctrines of religion, such as the reality of the invisible world. The general tendency of Satan's influence is delusion, yet he may mix some truth with his lies so that his lies may not be so easily discovered.

Thus multitudes are deluded with a counterfeit faith as a result of impressions that are made with their imagination. All their convictions of the truth of religion are merely based upon these imaginary visions and experiences.

Heightened emotional experiences may deceive. A third form of deception is when people depend upon a heightened experience in their interest of religion. They start having a confidence that if there is a Christ and heaven, both are theirs. This confidence in turn prejudices them more in favor of the truth of Christ's and heaven's existence. So when they hear of the great and glorious things of religion, they have the notion that all these things belong to them. They readily become overconfident that they are true. Hell is for other people, and heaven is certainly theirs. Confident that they are children of God and that God has promised heaven to them, they appear strong in the faith of their reality. They may even have great zeal against unbelief, yet the basis of their zeal is false.

VI. GRACIOUS AFFECTIONS FLOW FROM DEEP AWARENESS OF PERSONAL INSUFFICIENCY

Evangelical humiliation is a phrase that describes the Christian's sense of personal inadequacy, of his unworthiness, and his responsive attitude of heart to God in all his need.

Distinction may be drawn between legal and evangelical humiliation. The former is what men may be subject to when they are living in a natural state and have no gracious affections. The latter is a distinctive of true Christians. The former may arise from the common influence of the Spirit of God, especially as it is prompted by the natural conscience, but the latter is the distinctive influence of the Spirit of God who implants and exercises supernatural and divine principles. The former is the general sense of religious awe, such as the Israelites experienced when the attributes of God were revealed to them when the law was given at Mount Sinai. But the latter comes only from a personal sense of the transcendent beauty of divine things in their moral excellence. In the former the awful greatness and perfections of God, as well as the severity of His law, may convince men that they are exceedingly sinful and guilty, exposed to the wrath of God. However, they do not see their own unworthiness on account of sin, nor do they see the hateful nature of sin.

What is the difference between legal humiliation and evangelical humiliation?

A true sense of sin is only found in evangelical humiliation, in seeing for oneself the beauty of God's holiness and moral perfection. In legal humiliation, men are made aware that they are small, indeed nothing, before the great and terrible God. They feel undone, and wholly insufficient to help themselves. But they do not have a responsive frame of heart in true self-abasement nor do they feel the need to exult in God alone. This attitude comes only in evangelical humiliation, when the heart is overwhelmed by the realization of God's holy beauty. In a legal humiliation, the conscience is convicted, but there is still no spiritual understanding, nor is the will broken, nor is the inclination of the heart altered. Again this can only be done in evangelical humiliation. In legal humiliation, men are brought to self-despair in trying to help themselves. But in evangelical humiliation, they freely deny and renounce themselves. The one is forced while the other is a gentle yielding in freedom and delight to lie prostrate at the feet of God.

Only evangelical humiliation has a true sense of sin.

In itself legal humiliation has no spiritual value.

Thus legal humiliation has no spiritual value, while evangelical humiliation is a wonderful fruit of Christian grace. Legal humiliation is only useful when it leads to evangelical humiliation. Yet men may be legally humbled and still have no real humility, so the essence of evangelical humiliation consists in such humility as becomes an exceedingly sinful creature under the dispensation of grace. It is a low esteem of self, and sees self as indeed nothing, with no desire to feel self-sufficient, and freely renouncing all self-glory.

Without true humility there can be no true religion.

Humility, then, is the most essential thing in true religion. The whole setting of the gospel and everything that belongs to the New Covenant should have this effect upon the hearts of men. Without it there can be no true religion, whatever profession may be made and however intense the person's religious affections appear to be. "Behold, his soul which is lifted up is not upright in him; but the just shall live by his faith" (Habakkuk 2:4). That is to say, only he shall live who has faith in God's righteousness and grace rather than in his own goodness and excellence. God has abundantly shown in His Word that this is one of the distinctive features of His saints. Nothing else is acceptable to Him. "The Lord is nigh unto them that are of a broken heart, and saves such as be of a contrite spirit" (Psalm 34:18, cf. 51:17). "Although the Lord is high, yet has He respect unto the lowly" (Psalm 138:6). "He gives grace unto the lowly" (Proverbs 3:34).

Likewise in the New Testament we read, "Blessed are the poor in spirit; for theirs is the Kingdom of God" (Matthew 5:3). "Truly I say unto you, except you be converted and become as little children, you shall not enter into the Kingdom of Heaven. Whosoever therefore shall humble himself as this little child, the same is greatest in the Kingdom of Heaven" (Matthew 18:3, 4). In the story of the woman who anointed Jesus' feet with the precious box of ointment, in the Parable of the publican and the Pharisee, and in many other incidents in our Lord's life we see the emphasis that He makes on the need for humility.

If we make the Holy Scriptures our rule in judging the nature of true religion, then we must view humility as one of the most essential things that characterizes true Christianity.[1]

Humility is a key requisite of gracious affections.

The great Christian duty is self-denial. This duty consists in two things: first, in denying worldly inclinations and its enjoyments, and second, in denying self-exultation and renouncing one's self-significance by being empty of self. Self-renunciation must be done freely, from the heart. Then a Christian will have evangelical humiliation. This last is the more difficult part of self-denial, although the two go together. By renouncing the world and its common enjoyments, many Anchorites and Recluses have done the first, but they may not have done the second. Their spiritual pride or self-righteousness may still exalt them before God and above their fellow creatures.

What is true self-denial?

This humiliation is what even the most distinguished hypocrites, who may glory in their mortification to the world, deeply fail to have. For if they are not led by the Spirit, they will not be guided to have a behavior that is becoming of holy humility.

Some people are full of talk against legal doctrines, legal preaching, and the legal spirit. Yet they may understand very little of what they are talking against. A legal spirit is far more subtle than they imagine. It can lurk, operate, and prevail in their hearts even while they are inveighing against it. For as long as a man is not emptied of himself and of his own righteousness and goodness, he will have a legal spirit. A spirit of pride in one's own

How subtle is legalism?

---

[1]Calvin in his *Institutes* says: "I was always exceedingly pleased with that saying of Chrysostom, 'The foundation of our philosophy is humility'; and yet more pleased with that of Augustine: 'As,' says he, 'the rhetorician, being asked what was the first thing in the rules of eloquence, answered "pronunciation"; what was the second, "pronunciation"; what was the third, still he answered, "pronunciation!" ' So if you shall ask me concerning the precepts of the Christian religion, I would answer, firstly, secondly, and thirdly and forever, humility" (book 11, chapter 2, paragraph 11).

righteousness, morality, holiness, affection, experience, faith, humiliation, or any other goodness, is a legal spirit. In fallen man a legal spirit is nothing else but spiritual pride. He will trust this inherently and so recommend himself before God. With such encouragement he goes before God in prayer and expects much from God. He thinks this makes Christ love him and that Christ is willing to clothe him with His righteousness. He may even suppose that God is pleased with his experiences and graces, and yet all the while he is merely a deluded creature.

It is even possible to have a self-righteous spirit about one's own humility and to be self-confident about one's own abasement. It is the nature of spiritual pride to make men conceited and ostentatious about their humility.

How humble are the truly humble?

But to be truly emptied of self and to be poor in spirit and broken in heart is quite another matter. It is amazing how many are deceived about this, imagining themselves to be humble when they are proud and arrogant. The deceitfulness of man's heart is very apparent in spiritual pride and self-righteousness. Here the subtlety of Satan appears paramount. Perhaps one reason for this is his vast experience with it. Indeed it was his own sin. But despite its subtlety and secretiveness there are two ways in which spiritual pride or self-righteousness may be discovered and distinguished.

The truly humble do not compare themselves favorably.

It can be recognized when one compares himself to others when he thinks he is an eminent saint in comparison. This is the secret language of such a heart: "God, I thank You that I am not as other men" (Luke 18:11). "I am holier than you" (Isaiah 65:5). In taking the high place, they are doing what Christ condemns (Luke 14:7). They are confident that they are guides to the blind, but they are the blind in actuality (Romans 2:19, 20).

But he whose heart is subject to Christian humility has a very different attitude. For humility, or true lowliness of mind, causes people to think others better than themselves (Philippians 2:3). This is how Moses and Jeremiah viewed themselves, although they were eminent saints and had great knowledge (Exodus 3:11; Jeremiah 1:6). Humble people do not naturally think they are qualified to teach, but feel the need to be taught; they are much more eager to hear and to receive instructions than to dictate to others: "Swift to hear, slow to speak" (James 1:19). They are not likely to assume authority, but subject themselves to others. "Be not many masters" (James 3:1). "Clothed with humility" (1 Peter 5:5), they submit themselves "one to another in the fear of the Lord" (Ephesians 5:21).

There are some people who feel that all their experiences are extraordinary and wonderful; so they speak freely of the things that they have experienced. This may be a reasonable perception. For indeed it is infinitely wonderful that God should bestow the smallest crumb of the children's bread on such dogs as we. And so the humbler a person is, the more apt he is to call any mercy of God a wonderful thing. But if by wonderful things they mean a comparatively greater spiritual experience than others have experienced, then they are speaking with a form of pride. They assume that because they acknowledge that God has done it, they are not showing any sign of pride. But this is how the Pharisees spoke. In Luke 18 the Pharisee said, "God, I thank You that I am not as other men."[2] But a verbal recognition of the grace of God does not diminish their forwardness in thinking so highly of their own holiness. This then gives evidence of the pride and vanity of their minds.

The truly humble say little of their experiences.

If they were humble, their attainments in religion would not be apt to shine in their own eyes, nor would they admire their own beauty. Christians who are real saints and the greatest in the Kingdom of Heaven humble themselves as a little child (Matthew 18:4). They look upon themselves as children in grace, whose attainments

The truly humble are like little children.

---

[2]Calvin, in *Institutes*, speaking of this Pharisee, observes: "In his outward confession, he acknowledges that the righteousness that he has is the gift of God: but says he, because he trusts that he is righteous, he goes away out of the presence of God, unacceptable and odious" (book III, chapter 12, paragraph 7).

are only those of babes in Christ. They marvel and are ashamed of the low level of their love, gratitude, and knowledge of God. Moses, when he conversed with God on the mount, was unconscious that his face shone so brightly it dazzled the people. No eminent saint has any boast. He is more likely to consider himself to be the least of all saints and to think that every other saint's attainments and experiences are greater than his own.[3]

Lowliness thinks it is little because it sees what it ought to be. Likewise, any sanctity that a gracious soul has appears little compared with the greatness of what he sees before him. It is like the child of a great prince. He is jealous for the honor of his father, and sees the honor and respect that others show him as small and unworthy in comparison with the honor his father's dignity demands.

The truly humble have little sense of their own goodness.

True grace and spiritual light open up a person's view of God. The greater the view and sense that one has of the infinite excellence and glory of God in Christ, and of how boundless is the length and breadth, depth and height of the love of Christ to sinners, the greater will be the astonishment one feels as he realizes how little he knows of such love to such a God, and to such a glorious Redeemer. The more he sees this the more his own grace and love will diminish. It will amaze him to think that other saints would ever have as little grace as he has for the unspeakable love of Christ, who deserves so much more. He will be apt to see this as something peculiar to himself, for he can only see the outside of other Christians, but he sees only too well his own heart.

It may be argued that a person's love of God increases in proportion to his knowledge of God. If this is true, why does an increase in knowledge in a saint make his love ap-

---

[3]Luther, as he is quoted by Samuel Rutherford in *Spiritual Antichrist*, says: "So is the life of a Christian, that he that has begun, seems to himself to have nothing; he strives and presses forward that he may apprehend. Thus Paul says, I count not myself to have apprehended. . . . Likewise Bernard says, He is not a Christian that thinks he is a finished Christian and is insensible how far short he falls. . . . That man without doubt, has never so much as begun to be renewed, nor did he ever taste what it is to be a Christian" (pp. 143, 144).

pear to be less? I answer that it is not just simply a question of an increase of knowledge or the sight of God. For the more the vision of God grows in a saint, the more he is convinced there is much more to see. What is seen is indeed wonderful, but it brings a strong conviction of something that is vastly beyond. So the saint grows the more amazed at his own ignorance and how little he loves. He longs for a greater capacity to know. If only the clouds and darkness were removed. This causes the soul in enjoyment of a spiritual perspective to complain greatly of spiritual ignorance, the lack of love, and to long to experience more knowledge and more love.

Even in the most eminent saints are grace and the love of God small in comparison to what they ought to be. The highest love that can ever be reached in this life is poor, cold, trivial, and not worthy to be named in comparison to what our obligations really are. There are two reasons for this. First, God has given us reasons to love Him: in this revelation of His infinite glory in His Word, in His works, in the gospel of His Son, and in what He has done for sinful man. Second, God has given the soul of man the capacity to see and understand His love. Yet how small is the love of the most eminent saint in comparison to what God deserves!

The truly humble lament their own sinfulness.

When the saint compares his love with his obligations, he realizes how far short his love falls. He also sees not only how little he loves, but also how great is the corruption remaining within him. For sin is falling short of God's demands of us. The more the saints realize their inadequacy, the more they see how vile they are. Thus it appears to them that they are full of sin in not loving Christ enough. Before their eyes this is the most hateful ingratitude.

Saints tend also to emphasize their sinfulness as over any goodness they have. They see the least sin against an infinite God as an infinite perversion. They feel that the highest degree of their holiness does not have infinite loveliness. Therefore its loveliness is nothing in comparison with the ugliness of the least sin. The more spiritual light a person has, the more this attitude is intensified.

The humble see their sins more clearly.

Many religious people tend to hide and cover up the corruption of their own hearts so that they do not see themselves as they are before God. But the more eminent that saints are, the more they will have the light of heaven in their souls. Thus they will appear to themselves to be the more debased and sinful. They can only cover themselves with the righteousness of Christ, and allow their own deficiencies to be swallowed up and hid in the beams of His abundant glory and love. Yet how must our most ardent love and praises appear to the angelic beings who behold the beauty and glory of God ceaselessly? How does our deepest gratitude for the dying love of Christ appear to them who see Christ as He really is, who know as they are known, and see the glory of the One who died, and who gaze constantly at the wonders of His dying love without any cloud of darkness? No wonder the highest attainments of the saints on earth appear so mean to them. They dwell in the light of God's glory and they see God as He is.

The truly humble are the most freed of self.

At the same time I do not want to be understood to say that the more saints on earth experience God's grace, the lower will be the opinion of themselves. In many ways it is quite otherwise, for when grace is most exercised, there is proportionate freedom from the corruption of sin. They are freer from a sense of guilt than many who still have only a legal sense of sin. Yet it is also true that the children of God never have a more sensitive awareness of their own sinfulness than when they are most enjoying the true and pure grace of God. It is the greatest in the kingdom who humbles himself as the least infant among them (Matthew 18:4).

From this we may lay down an almost infallible rule, "That he who tends to think he is eminent compared with others, and more distinguished in Christian experience is bound to be mistaken. He is no eminent saint but merely living in the delusion of a proud and self-righteous spirit." If this is habitual with him and dominates his thinking, then he is no saint at all. Indeed, he shows that he has the least understanding of true Christian experience.

For the person who is blown up with self-conceit is demonstrating that he knows nothing of the nature of true spiritual light. The more spiritual knowledge a person has, the more he is sensible of his own ignorance. "He that thinks he knows anything, knows nothing as he ought to know" (1 Corinthians 8:2). When he made a great discovery of God, Agur sensed the wonder of His glory and of His marvellous works and cried out in a deep sense of his ignorance: "Surely I am more brutish than any man, and have not the understanding of a man. I neither learned wisdom, nor have the knowledge of the holy. Who has ascended up into heaven, or descended? Who has gathered the wind in his fists? Who has bound the waters in a garment? Who has established all the ends of the earth? What is his name, and what is his son's name, if you can tell?" (Proverbs 30:2-4).

The spiritually minded have no self-conceit.

A man who is highly convinced of his spiritual and divine knowledge is wise only in his own eyes. We are warned against this: "Be not wise in your own eyes" (Proverbs 3:7). "Be not wise in your own conceits" (Romans 12:16, cf. Isaiah 5:21). Experience then shows the truth of Proverbs 26:12: "Do you see a man wise in his own conceit? There is more hope of a fool than for him."

Some may object that the Psalmist, who we must suppose was in a holy frame of mind, speaks of his knowledge as eminently great and far greater than that of other saints. "I have more understanding than all my teachers: for your testimonies are my meditation. I understand more than the ancients, because I keep your precepts" (Psalm 119:99, 100). To this I make two points.

Why then did the Psalmist boast of his knowledge?

First, there is no restraint laid upon the Spirit of God as to what He may reveal to a prophet for the benefit of His Church while he is speaking or writing under immediate inspiration. The Spirit of God may reveal to him things that would otherwise be hard or impossible for him to find

The Holy Spirit reveals to whom He will.

out. For example, the Spirit of God might have revealed to David this distinguishing benefit that he had received by conversing much with God's testimonies, and then He used him as His instrument to record for the benefit of others.

The Psalmist's knowledge may have been of God's future purpose.

Second, it is not certain that the knowledge David speaks of here is the spiritual knowledge of which holiness fundamentally consists. It may be he is talking about a greater revelation which God had given to him of the Messiah and of the things concerning his future kingdom. This is given to him for keeping God's Word. In the Book of Psalms it is apparent that David far exceeded all who had gone before him in the knowledge of the mysteries and the doctrines of the gospel.

The truly humble are discontented with their spiritual accomplishments.

Another infallible sign of spiritual pride is when persons think highly of their humility. False experiences are commonly associated with a counterfeit humility. It is the very nature of false humility to be highly conceited about itself. False religious affections have the tendency, when they are intensified, to make people think that their humility is great and therefore they take notice of their great accomplishments in this area, and admire them. Whereas gracious affections have a contrary tendency, causing people to become deeply humble and to long earnestly after more humility. Their present humility appears small and their remaining pride great and disgusting.

Thus an eminent saint is not apt to think of himself as eminent in anything. All his graces and experiences will appear to him to be comparatively little, and especially his humility. Nothing that belongs to Christian experience and true piety is so much out of his sight as is his humility. He is a thousand times more discerning about his pride than about his humility. In contrast, the deluded hypocrite under the power of spiritual pride is so blind that he never sees his pride and yet is quick sighted about any show of humility within himself.

Again, the humble Christian is more apt to find fault
with his own pride than with that of other men. He is apt
to put the best construction on others' words and behavior
and to think that none is as proud as he is. But the proud
hypocrite is quick to discern the mote in his brother's eye.
He never sees the beam in his own. He is often crying out
about someone else's pride, finding fault with that person's appearance and way of living. Yet he never sees the
filthiness of his own heart.

The truly humble
see their own
pride most
clearly.

This tendency in hypocrites to think highly of their
own humility causes them to put their counterfeit humility on exhibition. As it was in the past with the false
prophets (Zechariah 13:4; Isaiah 57:5), a great show of
their humility is made. Likewise Christ tells us that the
Pharisees called attention to their fasting (Matthew
6:16). True humility does not make any display, nor is it
noisy. A true penitent is represented as still and silent.
"He sits alone and keeps silent, because he has borne it
upon himself" (Lamentations 3:28). Silence is often associated with humility. "If you have done foolishly in lift-
ing up yourself, or if you have thought evil, lay your hand
upon your mouth" (Proverbs 30:32).

A truly humble person who has a low view of his own
righteousness and holiness is poor in spirit. That is to say
he has a low view of himself and consequently has a com-
parable attitude. He will behave differently. "The poor
uses entreaties, but the rich answers roughly." A poor man
is not as likely to have a quick and strong resentment as a
rich man. He is also apt to yield to others, for he knows
others are better than he is. He is not obstinate and self-
willed. He is patient. He expects to be despised and so
takes it patiently. He is not upset when he is overlooked
and regarded lightly, for he is prepared to take a low position. He readily honors his superiors and takes reproof
quietly. He is docile in teaching. He does not claim much
for his own understanding and judgment. Although he is
unassuming, he is not servile. It is natural for him to be

The marks of the
truly humble

subject to others. This is the character of a humble Christian.

A poor man is a beggar; so is he that is "poor in spirit." There is a vast difference between those affections that are truly gracious and those that are false. Under the former the person will continue to be a poor beggar at God's gates, exceedingly empty and needy. But the latter makes men feel they are rich and increased with goods and in need of nothing.[4]

A poor man is modest in his speech and behavior; and especially so is one who is "poor in spirit." He is humble and modest in his behavior before men. It is vain for any to pretend that they are humble and as little children before God when they are haughty, assuming, and impudent in their behavior among men. The Apostle informs us that the purpose of the gospel is to cut off all glorying, not only before God, but also before men (Romans 4:1, 2). Some pretend to be humble but are still haughty, and they assume in their external appearances and behavior an audacious attitude. They need to consider what the Scriptures say about this. "Lord, my heart is not haughty, nor my eyes lofty; neither do I exercise myself in great matters, or in things too high for me" (Psalm 131:1). "These six things does the Lord hate; yea seven are an abomination unto Him: a proud look" (Proverbs 6:16, 17). "A high look, and a proud heart is sin" (Proverbs 21:4). "Him that has a high look and a proud heart, I will not suffer" (Psalm 101:5).

The attractive modesty of the humble.

Christian behavior that arises from humility has a certain attractive modesty and fear. The Scripture often speaks of it. "Be ready to give an answer to every man that asks you . . . with meekness and fear" (1 Peter 3:15). "While they behold your chaste conversation coupled with fear" (1 Peter 3:2). "That women adorn themselves

---

[4]"Truly reverend, when I see the curse of God upon many Christians that are now grown full of their parts, gifts, peace, comforts, abilities, duties, I stand adoring the riches of the Lord's mercies, through a little handful of poor believers, not only in making them empty, but in keeping them so all their days" (Shepard, *Sound Believer*, p. 159).

in modest apparel, with shamefacedness and sobriety"
(1 Timothy 2:9). In this respect a Christian is like a little
child, for a little child is modest before others and his
heart is apt to be possessed with a spirit of fear and awe
when he is among adults.

The same spirit will dispose a Christian to honor all
men. "Honor all men" (1 Peter 2:17). He will do so not
only in his behavior but in all those ways that do not imply
a visible approbation of sin. Thus Abraham, the great pa-
tron of believers, honored the children of Heth.
"Abraham stood up, and bowed himself to the people of
the land" (Genesis 23:7). Paul honored Festus in calling
him "most noble Festus" (Acts 26:25).

I have tried to describe the heart and behavior of one
who is governed by truly gracious humility, as the Scriptures describe. It is out of a heart such as this that all holy
affections flow. Christian affections are like the precious
ointment Mary poured on Christ's head, filling the house
with a sweet odor. These were poured out of an alabaster
box just as gracious affections flow out to Christ out of a
pure heart. The box it was poured from had to be broken
because until the box was broken the ointment could not
flow or diffuse its perfume. Similarly, gracious affections
flow out of a broken heart. All gracious affections that are
a sweet perfume to Christ and that fill the soul of a Christian with a heavenly sweetness and fragrance are brokenhearted affections.

> True affections flow from a humble heart.

Thus, truly Christian love, either to God or man, is a
humble brokenhearted love. The desires of the saints,
however earnest, are humble desires. Their hope is a
humble hope. Their joy even, when it is unspeakable and
full of glory, is a humble, brokenhearted joy that leaves
the Christian more poor in spirit, more like a little child,
and more disposed to humble behavior.

VII
GRACIOUS AFFECTIONS CHANGE US TO BE MORE CHRIST-LIKE

nother way in which gracious affections are distinguished is that they create a change of character. For true spiritual discoveries are life-changing and are more than temporary experiences. They are powerful enough to alter the very nature of the soul.

VII. GRACIOUS AFFECTIONS DEPEND UPON CONVERSIONS THAT CHANGE OUR CHARACTERS

"But we all with open face, beholding as in a glass the glory of the Lord, are changed into the same image, from glory to glory, even as by the Spirit of the Lord" (2 Corinthians 3:18). Such power as this is indeed divine, a distinctive of the Spirit of the Lord. Other powers can make changes in human temperaments and feelings. But it is the power of the Creator alone that can change the nature and give a new nature. No other means can make such a profound change in the soul.

This is the effect of true affections in conversion. The Scripture speaks of conversion as a change of nature. It uses metaphors such as being born again; becoming new creatures; rising from the dead; being renewed in the spirit of the mind; dying to sin and living to righteousness; putting off the old man, and putting on the new man; being

141

ingrafted in a new stock; having a divine seed implanted in the heart; being made partakers of the divine nature, and so on.

Conversion is not real without deep, abiding changes of life.

If there is no great and abiding change in people who think they have experienced a work of conversion, they are deluded.[1] In turning from sin to God, a converted man experiences a great and universal change. A man may be restrained from sin before he is converted. But when he is converted, he is not only restrained from sin, but his very heart and nature are turned away from it toward a life of holiness. If, therefore, there is little evidence of any change in his bad habits and dispositions, then he may well question the reality of his conversion.

Allowances must be made for our temperaments.

Yet allowances must be made for our natural temperaments. Conversion does not entirely root out our natural dispositions. For those sins toward which a man is naturally inclined before his conversion will still be the ones that he is apt to fall into. Nevertheless, conversion makes a great change even in respect to these failings because even though grace is received imperfectly and so does not root out all of the evil in the natural temperament, it still has great power and efficacy. The change brought by conversion is radical, changing whatever is sinful in a person's life. The old man is put off, and a new man is put on. Sanctified throughout, the person becomes a whole new being. Converting grace makes a great change in his evil dispositions. He may still be tempted by such, but his temptations will no longer have dominion over him.

We cannot rely upon our feelings.

Some, relying foolishly upon their feelings for God, argue that when their feelings and affections for God disappear, their conversion now means nothing. In despair they feel God has left them. They are tempted to feel and think they are no better than they used to be.

---

[1] "I would not judge of the whole soul's coming to Christ, so much by sudden pangs as by inward bent. For the whole soul in affectionate expressions and actions may be carried to Christ; but being without this change of disposition and affections, it is unsound." (Shepard, *Parable of the Ten Virgins*, part 1, p. 203).

It is very true that all grace and goodness in the hearts of true Christians are entirely from God. They are completely dependent upon Him for them. Yet these saints may be mistaken about how God may communicate Himself by His Spirit in saving grace. God gives life, not just something additional. Christ lives in the soul. So grace in the soul is as much from Christ as the light in a prism is from the sun. The glass remains as it was; its nature does not change, and yet the light is received. This only partially represents the communication of grace to the soul. But the true Christian receives light from the Son of Righteousness in such a way that his nature is changed, and becomes like the light received. God's people become like little suns. To change the metaphor, they not only drink of the water of life flowing from the original fountain, but this water becomes a fountain within them, springing and flowing out of them (John 4:14; 7:38, 39).

Conversion is a lifelong change of life.

The spiritual insights and affections first experienced in conversion are transforming. They reach down to the bottom of the heart, affecting and altering the very nature of the soul. But the process of transformation is continued and carried on to the end of life, until it is brought to perfection and glory. This progress of the work of grace in the hearts of God's people is represented in Scripture as a continued conversion and renovation of nature.

Reflecting this truth, the Apostle exhorts those that were in Rome, "the beloved of God, called to be saints" and so "to be transformed by the renewing of their mind" (Romans 12:1, 2). Likewise, the Apostle writes to the "saints and faithful in Christ Jesus that are at Ephesus" (Ephesians 1:1) "who were once dead in trespasses and sins, who were now quickened and raised up and made to sit together in heavenly places in Christ and created in Christ Jesus unto good works." He exhorts these same persons "to put off the old man, which is corrupt according to the deceitful lusts; and be renewed in the spirit of their minds; and put on a new man, which after God is created in righteousness and true holiness" (Ephesians 4:22-24).

Gracious affec-
tions are lasting.   Some affections do not last. They disappear, leaving a
void. But this is not so with true, gracious affections.[2]
They leave a lingering perfume and a stronger inclination
toward holy living before God. In his remarkable en-
counter with God, Moses' face did not only shine while he
was on the mount, but it continued to shine afterwards as
well. When people have been conversing with Christ in
some remarkable way, an abiding impact is seen. Their
demeanor is affected because they have been with Jesus
(Acts 4:13).

VIII. Gracious Affections Have Christ-Like Gentleness

In contrast to false and delusive affections, truly gracious affections are associated with the gentle spirit of
Jesus Christ. Like the lamb and the dove, they promote a
spirit of love, meekness, quietness, forgiveness, and
mercy as seen in Christ.

Evidence of this in Scripture is abundant. If we judge
the true nature of Christianity and the proper spirit of the
gospel by the Word of God, this may well be called the
Christian spirit. It is the distinguishing disposition in the
hearts of Christians to be identified as Christians.

When some of the disciples spoke in weakness and in-
consideration, Christ reprimanded them saying they
knew not of what manner of spirit they were (Luke 9:55).
He implied that theirs was not the proper spirit of His
kingdom. But all who are truly godly and are real disciples
of Christ have a gentle spirit in them. This spirit so possesses and governs them that it becomes their true and
proper character. This is evident by what the wise man
says: "A man of understanding is of an excellent spirit"
(Proverbs 17:27). Christ, when he describes the qualities

---

[2] "Do you think the Holy Spirit comes on a man as on Balaam, by immediate
striving and then leaves him so that he has nothing?" (Shepard, *Parable of the
Ten Virgins*, p. 1, p. 126).

and temper of those that are truly blessed, says, "Blessed are the meek: for they shall inherit the earth. Blessed are the merciful: for they shall obtain mercy. Blessed are the peacemakers: for they shall be called the children of God" (Matthew 5:5, 7, 9).

This spirit is a distinctive character of the elect of God, as seen in Colossians 3:12, 13: "Put on therefore as the elect of God, holy and beloved, bowels of mercies, kindness, humbleness of mind, meekness, long-suffering; forbearing one another, and forgiving one another." The Apostle speaks of this Christ-like disposition as the most excellent and essential thing in Christianity. None are true Christians without it. Their vaunted professions and gifts are nothing without it (cf. 1 Corinthians 13).

None are true Christians without being Christ-like.

The same Apostle in Galatians 5 specifically declares the distinguishing marks and truths of true Christian grace consist chiefly in those things that have the spirit and temper I have been describing. "The fruit of the Spirit is love, joy, peace, long-suffering, gentleness, goodness, faith, meekness, temperance" (vv. 22, 23). Likewise the Apostle James asserts the same truth (James 3:14-17).

All that belongs to holiness of heart is the very nature of true Christianity. It is the character of Christians. But it is the spirit of holiness itself that is the distinguishing trait of the Christians. Christians also have attractive qualities and virtues that correspond particularly with the nature of the gospel and of the Christian witness. These relate to the divine attributes which God has so wonderfully shown and glorified in the work of redemption by Jesus Christ, which is the great subject of Christian revelation. These are virtues such as humility, meekness, love, forgiveness and mercy.

It is the Spirit of holiness.

These qualities also distinguish the character of Jesus Christ Himself, the great Head of the Christian Church. They are often spoken of in the prophesies of the Old Testament. We read in Matthew 21:5: "Tell you the daughter of Zion, behold your king comes unto you, meek, and

Jesus is gentle.

sitting upon an ass." So Christ describes Himself: "Learn of Me, for I am meek and lowly in heart" (Matthew 11:29). That is why He is often called the Lamb in Scripture. Since such traits so distinctively describe Christ, real Christians bear the same characteristics. "The new man is renewed, after the image of Him that created him" (Colossians 3:10; cf. 2 Corinthians 3:10; 1 Corinthians 15:47, 48).

Christians must be gentle, too. Christians are followers of Christ and are therefore obedient to His call. "Come to Me, and learn of Me: for I am meek and lowly in heart" (Matthew 11:28, 29). They are those who follow the Lamb wherever He goes (Revelation 14:4). True Christians are those who are clothed with the meek, quiet, and loving spirit of Christ. When they are in Christ, they have put on Christ. This is the very nature of the Christian spirit as evidenced by the dove, God's chosen symbol. The Spirit who descended on Christ when He was anointed of the Father descended on Him like a dove, a noted emblem of meekness, harmlessness, peace, and love. It is the same spirit who descended upon the Head of the Church that descends on its members. "God has sent forth the Spirit of His Son into their hearts" (Galatians 4:6).

Meekness is so characteristic of the saints that *meek* and *godly* are used as synonymous terms in Scripture. In Psalm 37:10, 11 the wicked and the meek are set in contrast to each other. Again, "The Lord lifts up the meek: he casts the wicked down to the ground" (Psalm 147:6).

Christians have the qualities of little children. Christ represents all His disciples, all the heirs of heaven, as little children for doubtlessly the same reason. "Suffer little children to come unto Me, and forbid them not; for such is the Kingdom of Heaven" (Matthew 19:14; cf. Matthew 10:42; 18:6, 10, 14; John 13:33). Little children are innocent and harmless so men do not need to be afraid of them. This should be true of Christians (1 Corinthians 14:20). Little children are not full of guile and deceit, but are plain and simple because they are not versed in the arts of fiction and deceit. They are flexible, not willful and obstinate. They do not trust their own understanding, but rely on the instruction of parents and of others of superior understanding. Children are therefore a fit and living symbol of the followers of the Lamb. Child-likeness is not only a highly commendable trait to have, but it is also an essential one. "Truly I say unto you, except to be converted, and to become as little children, you shall not enter into the Kingdom of Heaven" (Matthew 18:3; cf. Mark 10:15).

But some may be ready to object and say, is there no such thing as Christian fortitude and boldness for Christ? Should we not be good soldiers in Christian warfare and come out boldly against the enemies of Christ and His people?

What then of manly qualities?

Of course there is. The whole Christian life is compared to a warfare, and fitly so. The most distinguished Christians are the best soldiers, those endued with the greatest fortitude. It is the duty of God's people to be steadfast and strong in their opposition to the designs and ways that would overthrow the Kingdom of Christ and His interests. Yet many people seem to be quite mistaken concerning the nature of Christian fortitude. It is quite the opposite of brutal fierceness such as the boldness of beasts of prey. Rather, true Christian fortitude consists of a strength of mind, through grace. This is exerted in two ways. It overrules and suppresses evil, unruly passions and affections of the mind. And it exerts steadfastly and freely good affections and dispositions without being hampered by sinful fear or the opposition of enemies.

The character of true fortitude

The real strength of the good soldier of Jesus Christ is simply the steadfast maintenance of a holy calmness, meekness, sweetness, and a benevolence of mind that is sustained amidst all the storms, injuries, wrong behavior, and unexpected acts and events in this evil and unreasonable world. The Scripture seems to intimate that true fortitude consists chiefly of this: "He that is slow to anger, is better than the mighty; and he that rules his spirit, than he that takes a city" (Proverbs 16:32).

In order to see the true nature of holy fortitude that

should be evident when fighting with God's enemies, one needs to look at the Captain of all God's hosts. See our great leader and example. See how He has fought and won His glorious victories. Look then at Jesus Christ at the time of His last Passion when all His enemies on earth and hell made their most violent attack upon Him, encompassing Him on every side like roaring lions. How did He show His boldness and valor at that time? Not in fiery passions, nor fierce and violent speeches, but simply in His silence. For He went "as a lamb to the slaughter, and as a sheep before His shearers was dumb."

He also displayed fortitude in praying that the Father would forgive His enemies because they knew not what they did. He did not shed others' blood, but with all conquering patience and love, He shed His own. Indeed, one of His disciples made a pretense to be bold for Christ, and confidently declared he would sooner die with Christ than deny Him. He began to swing about with a sword. But Christ meekly rebuked him and healed the wound he gave. Never was the patience, meekness, love, and forgiveness of Christ so gloriously seen as it was on this occasion.

When people are fierce and violent, exerting sharp and bitter passions, they show weakness instead of strength and fortitude. "And I, brethren, could not speak unto you as unto spiritual, but as unto carnal, even as unto babes in Christ. For you are yet carnal: for whereas there is among you envy, and strife, and divisions, are you not carnal and walk as men?" (1 Corinthians 3:1-3).

False boldness for Christ   There is a false boldness for Christ that only comes from pride. A man may rashly expose himself to the world's dislike and even deliberately provoke its displeasure, and yet do so out of pride. It is the nature of spiritual pride to prompt men to seek distinction and singularly. Many times they will be militant with those they call carnal in order to be more highly exalted among their own party. True boldness for Christ transcends all, it is indifferent to the displeasure of either friends or foes. Boldness enables Christians to forsake all rather than Christ, and to prefer to offend all rather than to offend Him. So the Apostle did not seek glory as he declares in 1 Thessalonians 2:6).[3] Instead, such are bold for Christ and open about their faults.

Mistaken about real boldness for Christ, some will also be mistaken about Christian zeal. Zeal is like a burning flame against things. It is not against people; it is against evil. Bitterness against people is not a part of holy zeal. It is contrary to it. The warmer true zeal is, and the higher it is raised, the farther it is from bitterness. For it is the fervor of Christian love. Its opposition is primarily against evil things in a person, not against the person. Therefore true Christian zeal is not contrary to the spirit of meekness, gentleness, and love, the spirit of a little child, a lamb, or a dove, that have been spoken of. It is entirely compatible with them and tends to promote them.

True zeal is meekness for God.

The Christian spirit I have been describing is exercised in three things, namely forgiveness, love, and mercy. Note that Scripture is very clear about these and insists on the absolute necessity of having them as the tone and character of every Christian.

Christ refers to forgiveness as both negative and positive evidence concerning the character of a Christian. If we do not have a forgiving spirit, then we are not forgiven of God. Our Lord's teaching emphasizes the special attention we should give it, always bearing this in mind. "Forgive us our debts as we forgive our debtors. . . . For if you forgive men their trespasses, your Heavenly Father will also forgive you. But if you forgive not men their trespasses, neither will your Father forgive your trespasses" (Matthew 6:12, 14, 15). Christ expresses the same truth elsewhere (Mark 11:25, 26; Matthew 18:35).

The spirit of forgiveness.

---

[3]Mr. Shepard, speaking of hypocrites affecting applause, says: "Hence men forsake their friends, and trample under foot the scions of the world: they have credit elsewhere. To maintain their interests in the love of godly men, they will suffer much" (Shepard, *Parable of the Ten Virgins*, part 1, p. 180).

The spirit of kindness and love

The Scriptures also plainly and abundantly teach that all true saints have a loving, compassionate, and kind spirit. Without this, says the Apostle, we may speak with the tongues of men and angels yet we are only a sounding brass or a tinkling cymbal. Although we have the gift of prophesy, and understand all mysteries, and all knowledge, without this spirit we are nothing. No other virtue or disposition of mind is more often and expressly insisted upon as a mark of a true Christian. Love is often given as the evidence of who are Christ's disciples, and how they may be known.

Indeed, Christ calls the law of love His commandment. "A new commandment give I unto you, that you love one another; as I have loved you, that you also love one another" (John 13:34). "This is My commandment, that you love one another as I have loved you" (John 15:12). And verse 17, "These things I command you, that you love one another." He says in chapter 13:35, "By this shall all men know that you are My disciples, if you have love one to another." Again in chapter 14:21, "He that has My commandments, and keeps them, he it is that loves Me."

The beloved disciple who had so much of this loving spirit himself often insists upon its consistent practice. Indeed, he emphasizes this more than anything else and more than any other apostle as a sign of grace in those who profess to be Christians. "He that says he is in the light, and hates his brother, is in darkness even until now. He that loves his brother abides in the light, and there is no occasion of stumbling in him" (1 John 2:9, 10). "We know that we have passed from death unto life, because we love the brethren: he that loves not his brother abides in death" (3:14). "My little children, let us not love in word and in tongue, but in deed and truth. And hereby we know that we are of the truth, and assure our hearts before Him" (3:18, 19). And so he goes on in verses 23, 24, and in chapter 4:7, 8, 12, 13, 16, 20.

The spirit of compassion

The rest of Scripture is as plain as it could be about this. None are true saints except those who have the true character of compassion and concern to relieve the poor, indigent, and afflicted. "The righteous shows mercy and gives" (Psalm 37:21). "He is ever merciful, and lends" (verse 26). "He that honors God, has mercy on the poor" (Proverbs 14:31). "The righteous gives, and spares not" (Proverbs 21:26). "Pure religion and undefiled before God and the Father is this, to visit the fatherless and widows in their afflictions" (James 1:27). See also such passages as Hosea 6:6; Matthew 5:7; 2 Corinthians 8:8; James 2:13-16; 1 John 3:17; Matthew 25; and Isaiah 57:1.

Of course, even true Christians still have remnants of a contrary spirit and may even be guilty of behavior offensive to such a spirit. But this I affirm, there are no true Christians who live in the prevailing power of such a spirit so that it becomes truly their character. The Scripture speaks of no real Christians who have an ugly, selfish, angry, and contentious spirit. Nothing can be more contradictory than a morose, hard, closed, and spiteful Christian.

The Christian's Spirit is Christ's Spirit.

Yet allowances must be made for our natural human temperament with regard to this as well as to other things. If those who were once wolves and serpents are now converted, there is a remarkable change in their spirit even though it is not yet complete. Yes, indeed there is brought about the grace of the gospel that alters the former self. "The wolf shall dwell with the lamb, and the leopard shall lie down with the kid . . . the sucking child shall play on the hole of the asp, and the weaned child shall put his hand on the cockatrice's den. They shall not hurt or destroy in all my holy mountain. For the earth shall be full of the knowledge of the Lord, as the waters cover the sea" (Isaiah 11:6-9; cf. Isaiah 65:25).

So conversion implies a change of temperament.

We see that in the early church converts were remarkably changed. "For we ourselves were sometimes foolish, disobedient, deceived, serving diverse lusts and pleasures, living in malice and envy, hateful and hating one another. But after that the kindness and love of God our Savior toward man appeared, He saved us by the washing of regeneration, and renewing of the Holy Ghost (Titus 3:3-5). And in Colossians 3:7, 8 we read, "In which you also sometimes walked, when you lived in them. But now you also put off all these: anger, wrath, malice, blasphemy, filthy communication out of your mouth."

IX. Gracious Affections Soften the Heart in Christian Tenderness

False affections, even when people seem to be deeply affected by them while they are still fresh, tend to harden the heart. These affections tend to develop certain kinds of passion that are self-seeking, self-exalting, and in opposition to others. Such false affections, with their associated delusions, eventually stupify the mind and exclude those affections that have tenderness of heart. The result is that people become less affected by their present and past sins, and less sensitive of the possibility of future sins. They are less moved by the warnings and cautions of God's Word and by God's providential chastisements. They become more careless in heart and in their behavior, and less discerning about what is sinful. Evil no longer frightens them as it did when they feared hell. So they become careless in duties and negligent of unpleasant tasks.

Those whose affections are false tend to spoil and to yield more easily to temptations and indulge in lusts. They are far less careful of their behavior when they come into the holy presence of God. Indifferent to the cross, they assume there is no need to fear hell and so they relax in their ease and lusts.

A Savior from sin is much more than a Savior of sins. Instead of embracing Christ as their Savior from sin, such people trust Him as a Savior of their sins. Instead of flying to Him as their refuge from their spiritual enemies, they manipulate Him to defend them from their enemies, from God, and even to strengthen them against Him. To strengthen their self-interest, they make Christ the servant of sin and the vicegerent of the devil. Without fear and eventually without restraints, they would use Him against His own most solemn warnings and threatenings. They actually trust in Christ to allow them to quietly enjoy their sins and to defend them from God's displeasure. While they come close to Him, even to His bosom, they come to fight against Him.[4] However, some even make a great show of their love for God; they talk of His favor and suggest they have great joy in His love.

They are like those described by the Apostle Jude. Ungodly men, they turned the grace of God into lasciviousness (Jude 4). They trust in self-righteousness simply to accommodate themselves to His promise that the righteous shall live and are saved. "When I shall say to the righteous he shall surely live; if he trust in his own righteousness, and commit iniquity, all his righteousness shall not be remembered, but for his iniquity that he has committed, he shall die for it" (Ezekiel 33:13).

How different are gracious affections. They turn a heart of stone more and more into a gentle heart. The influence of holy love and hope is vastly more effective upon the heart, making it tender and filling it with a dread of sin or whatever else might displease or offend God. Also the heart is made to keep vigil and yet without a slavish fear of hell. Gracious affections, as we have seen, flow out of a contrite heart that is bruised and broken with godly sorrow.

Gracious affections are gentle.

The tender heart of a true Christian is vividly illustrated by our Savior when He compares it to a little child. The flesh of this child is very tender as is the heart of one who is newly born again. This is illustrated by Naaman's being cured of leprosy when he washed in Jordan. This is a

Gracious affections are child-like.

---

[4]"These are hypocrites that believe, that fail with regard to the use of the gospel, and of the Lord Jesus. We read of these in Jude 4, as men that turned grace into wantonness. For it is in this that the exceeding evil of man's heart appears, that not only the law, but also the glorious gospel of the Lord Jesus works in him in a manner that is unrighteous. It is all too common for men at the work of conversion to cry for grace and Christ, and then afterwards grow licentious, living in the breach of the law, and making their excuse for this the very gospel!" (Shepard, *Parable of the Ten Virgins,* part 1, p. 126).

type of the renewing of the soul that is washed in the laver of regeneration. "His flesh came again like the flesh of a little child" (2 Kings 5:14).

The mind of a little child is also tender. His heart is easily moved and influenced. This is true of a Christian in regard to spiritual things. As a small child readily sympathizes and weeps with them that weep because he cannot bear to see others in distress, so does the Christian (John 11:35; Romans 12:15; 1 Corinthians 12:26). A small child is easily won by kindness, and so is a Christian. A small child will grieve readily over temporal evils, and weep with his heart melted. A Christian, whose heart is sensitive to the evil of sin, should respond the same. Again, a small child is easily frightened by the appearance of outward evils or any threat to harm him, and so he flies to his parents' protection. A Christian should be alarmed at any appearance of moral evil or anything that threatens the hurt of the soul and fly to Christ. A child and a saint are thus both sensible of danger, afraid to be alone and distant from God. "Happy is the man that fears always; but he that hardens his heart shall fall into mischief" (Proverbs 28:14).

As a small child tends to be afraid of its superiors, dreading their anger, trembling at their frowns and threats, so is a true saint when he comes to God. "My flesh trembles for fear of You, and I am afraid of Your judgments" (Psalm 119:120). "To this man will I look, even to him that is poor, and trembles at My Word" (Isaiah 66:2). As a small child approaches superiors with awe, so the saint approaches God with holy awe and reverence. "Shall not His glory make you afraid? And His dread fall upon you?" (Job 13:11). Holy fear then is so much the nature of true godliness that the latter is identified in Scripture as "the fear of the Lord."

Gracious affections do not tend to make men forward, cocky, noisy, or boastful. Rather, they cause men to speak with trembling (Hosea 13:1). They clothe their behavior before God and man with holy fear (see Psalm 2:11; 1 Peter 3:15; 2 Corinthians 7:15; Ephesians 6:5; 1 Peter 3:2; Romans 11:20).

But some may argue, what about having a holy boldness in prayer and in the duties of divine worship? I reply
that doubtless there can be such an attitude and it is found
chiefly in devout saints who have high degrees of faith and
love. But this holy boldness is not the opposite of reverence but of discord and servility. It helps to remove moral
distance or alienation, such as a slave experiences. None
approach God with more fear and reverence than the
spotless and glorious angels in heaven who cover their
faces before His throne (Isaiah 6). Elijah, that great
prophet who had so much holy intimacy with God, when
he conversed with Him on the mount and was especially
near to Him, wrapped his face in his mantle. This was not
because he was terrified with any servile fear from the
great wind, earthquake, or fire. But after these were all
over, God spoke to him as a friend in a still small voice
(1 Kings 19:12, 13). Moses, with whom God spoke face
to face as a man speaks with his friend and who was distinguished from all the prophets in his intimacy with God,
reacted likewise. "He made haste, and bowed his head toward the earth, and worshiped" (Exodus 34:8).

In the seventh chapter of Luke we read of that woman
who approached Christ in humble modesty, reverence,
and shame when she stood at His feet, weeping behind
Him because she was not fit to appear before His face. Instead "she washed His feet with her tears" (verse 47).[5]

One reason why gracious affections are associated with
this spirit of tenderness is that true grace tends to promote
convictions of conscience. Before having experiences of
grace, people are apt to have a guilty conscience. After
conversion the sense of guilt may be removed, but one's
sensitivity to sin will be intensified. The heart will grow in
tenderness.

All gracious affections have a tendency to promote this
Christian tenderness of heart, not only with godly sorrow,
but also with a gracious joy. "Serve the Lord with fear, and

*Gracious affec-
tions are tender.*

---

[5]Dr. Ames, in his *Cases of Conscience,* speaks of a holy modesty in the worship of God as one sign of true humility (book 3, chapter 4, pp. 53, 54).

rejoice with trembling" (Psalm 2:11). Indeed, confident and assured hope that is truly gracious has this tendency. For the higher that holy hope is raised, the more there is Christian tenderness. The more servile fear is banished by holy assurance, the more there is the spirit of reverential fear, and the more one tends to be unafraid of natural evils because of trust in God. The less afraid one therefore is of bad news, the more one will tend to be sensitive to moral evil or sin. The more holy boldness one has, the less self-confidence one will have, and the more modesty. Such a person will be less shaken in faith, yet more moved by God's solemn warnings. Such a one has the firmest comfort, but the softest heart; richer than others in character, but the poorest of all in spirit. For the tallest and the strongest saint is the least and is as the tenderest child.

VIII
GRACIOUS AFFECTIONS ARE BALANCED, YET DYNAMIC IN GROWTH

nother way in which gracious and holy affections are contrasted with false ones is by their beautiful symmetry and proportion.

X. GRACIOUS AFFECTIONS ARE CONSISTENT AND CONSTANT

Not that this balance of virtues and of gracious affections of the saints in this life is perfect. Often it has defects because of a lack of grace, or lack of proper instruction, or from errors in judgment, or a temperamental defect, or a lack of education, or some other disadvantage. Yet there is none of the gross imbalance that is commonly observed in false religion.

Truly holy affections in a saint are balanced. This is the dominant trait of their sanctity. The whole image of Christ is impressed upon them. They have put off the old man and have put on the new man throughout. It has pleased the Father that in Christ all fulness should dwell, so there is in Him every grace; and He is full of grace and truth. "Of His fulness have they received grace for grace" (John 1:14, 16). Thus there is apparent in some saints the

Jointliness is well-balanced.

157

same beautiful proportion that there is in the true image of
Christ.

Hypocrites, in contrast, are like Ephraim of old of
whom God complained greatly, saying: "Ephraim is a cake
not turned" (Hosea 7:8). Or as we would say, he is half-
baked, without consistency in his affections. Such tend to
have strong qualities in some things, and none at all in
others. But with true affections there is balance so that
holy hope and holy fear go together in the saints. This is
observed in some of the Psalms (Psalms 33:18; 147:11).
So too, joy and holy fear go together (Matthew 28:8). But
one of the great differences between saints and hypocrites
is this, the joy and comfort of the saint are associated with
godly sorrow and mourning for sin. We see this in Ezekiel
20:42, 43, and 16:61-63. A true saint did not have godly
sorrow before he was born again, but since then he has
often expressed it. He is described in the beatitude of
Matthew 5:4, "Blessed are they that mourn, for they shall
be comforted."

**False Christians
are unbalanced.**   In hypocrites there is often an essential deficiency in
the various kinds of religious affections as well as an imbalance and strange partiality in these affections. For example, some make hard pretenses and a great show of their
love of God in Christ. It may be that they are greatly affected by what they have heard or thought concerning
God. Yet at the same time, they may not have a spirit of
benevolence and love toward those who are disposed to
contention, envy, revenge, and evil speaking. They may
allow a grudging spirit to remain inside them against a
neighbor for seven years or even double that time. They
may live with resentment and bitterness of spirit so they
do not practice the rule: "Doing unto others as you would
have it done unto you." On the other hand, there are
others who may show a great deal of kindness toward
others in a good-natured and generous way, yet have no
love for God.

Some are effusive with affections toward others. But
their love is restrictive, unlike true Christian love. They
may be full of affection for some people, and yet full of bit-

terness toward others. They may be closely knit with their own group, loving and admiring them, and yet in fierce opposition and dislike toward others. The admonition is: "Be like your Father which is in heaven; for He makes His sun to rise upon the evil and the good. For if you love them which love you, what reward do you have? Do not even the publicans do the same?" (Matthew 5:45, 46).

The inconsistency of pseudolove

Again, some may be very inconsistent in the character of their love for others as far as outer things are concerned. Generous and liberal with their worldly goods, they have no concern for the souls of men. Others may pretend to have a great love for men's souls, but have no compassion or charity toward their practical needs. The making of a great show of love, or pity, or distress for souls costs them nothing. Whereas to show mercy practically, they must part with some of their money. But true Christian love for our brethren extends both to the soul and to the body. This is like the love and compassion of Jesus Christ who showed mercy for men's souls by preaching the gospel to them, but who also showed mercy for their physical needs. He went about doing good, healing all manner of sickness and diseases among them. (See Mark 9:35.)

The inconsistency of being critical of others' weaknesses

Another imbalance appears when people are much offended by bad qualities in their fellow Christians, such as coldness or lifelessness, but at the same time are not affected by their own personal defects and weaknesses. A true Christian will mourn for both situations and be quick to discern his own defects as well.

The inconsistency of not trusting God in material things

As a general rule, I have observed, that it is a sign of pretense if people say they have reached high attainments in religion, yet have never reached lesser attainments. Or perhaps they pretend not to be afraid to venture their souls upon Christ and to commit all they are to Him in trusting His Word for their eternal welfare. Yet, at the same time they do not have enough confidence in God to trust Him with a little of their material well-being for charitable purposes. Such pretense is false.

What is true of the affections of love can also be observed in other religious affections. Those affections that are true will always have balance and proportion. For example, there are some who with great zeal and unaccountable concern exhort others and declare what they experience. At the same time they may have no inclination to do the things that are as important or are more important for real Christians to desire. For example, true Christians long to pour out their souls before God in secret, earnest prayer and praise to Him, seeking to live more for His glory and to be more conformed to Him. We read in Scripture of "groanings that cannot be uttered," and of longing, thirsting, and panting for God.

The marks of false zeal

Hatred and zeal will be balanced as well. When these come from right principles, they are generally against sin. "I hate every false way" (Psalm 119:104, cf. v. 128). But a false hatred and zeal against sin is merely against some particular sin. In this respect we may appear to be very zealous, and yet at the same time overlook some deeper weaknesses. False zeal is against the sins of others while having no zeal against their own sins. He who has true zeal exercises it chiefly against his own sins. Again, some pretend to have a great abhorrence of their own sinful hearts, and yet make light of sins practiced. They commit them apparently without much restraint or remorse.

The instability of pseudo-Christians

There is instability and inconsistency in the life of hypocrites. True Christians are those who "follow the Lamb wherever He goes." The righteous man is truly said to be one whose heart is fixed, trusting in God (Psalm 112:7), having his heart established with grace (Hebrews 13:9), and maintaining his way (Job 17:9). People whose religion is false practice their faith in fits and starts. Suddenly they rise, only suddenly to fall again, becoming quite careless and worldly. They are like the waters that pour down in a shower of rain so that the brook rushes abundantly for a short time and then becomes quite dry. With another shower, it flows again. A true saint is like a stream fed from a living spring which, though it may be greatly increased by a shower of rain and diminished in a time of drought, runs constantly. "The water that I shall give him shall be in him a well of water springing up" (John 4:14). Or it is like a tree that is planted by a stream that has a constant supply of water at the roots, so it is always green, even in time of the greatest drought (Jeremiah 17:7, 8). In contrast, hypocrites may be likened to comets that appear in the sky briefly with a mighty blaze, and then disappear (Jude 13). True saints are like fixed stars which, though they rise and set and even are obscured by the clouds, remain fixed in their course and may be truly said to shine with a constant light.

Their environment will influence the affections of people with false affections.

True Christians enjoy both fellowship and solitude.

Some are greatly affected when they are in the company of others, but have no such emotions when they are alone in prayer, in meditation, or conversing alone with God and separated from all the world.[1] But a true Christian can delight in religious fellowship and conversation, yet he also delights to retire from all fellow men and converse with God in solitude. This has the special advantage of fixing his heart and gauging his affections. True religion inclines people to be alone for holy meditation and prayer. It was so with Isaac (Genesis 24:63). It was much more so in the case of Jesus Christ. How often we read of His retiring to the mountains and solitary places for holy conversation with His Father! It is difficult to conceal great affections, yet gracious affections are of a much more silent and secret nature than those that are counterfeit.

They sorrow for others and also rejoice.

Saints sorrow for their own sins. They do this apart from their companions (Zechariah 12:12-14). Gracious joys, too, are like "hidden manna" (Revelation 2:17).

---

[1]"They have a name to live and that is enough though their hearts are dead" (Shepard, *Parable of the Ten Virgins*, part 1, p. 180). "The hypocrite is not for the closet, but for the synagogue" (Matthew 6:5, 6), (Flavel, *Touchstone of Sincerity*, chapter 7, section 2). Dr. Ames speaks of sincerity "As the character of persons who are obedient in absence, as well as in the presence of spectators; in secret as well as, indeed more than, in public" (*Cases of Conscience*, book 3, chapter 5).

True Christians
love to be quiet
and silent before
God.

The Psalmist speaks of his sweetest comforts as those
that were to be had in secret (Psalm 63:5, 6). Christ calls
His spouse away from the world into a retreat so He may
give her His sweetest love (Song of Solomon 7:11, 12). In
Scripture the best blessings the saints obtained were in
their retirement. God made His covenant with Abraham
when he was alone. It was the same with Isaac when he received Rebecca as a special gift from God. It was when
Jacob was retired for secret prayer that the Lord came to
him and he wrestled with Him until he obtained the blessing. God revealed Himself to Moses when he was in a solitary place in the desert (Exodus 3). Again, later, God
showed Moses His glory and admitted him to the highest
degree of communion with God that he ever enjoyed.
This was when he was alone on the mountain for forty
days and nights. It was when they were in retirement that
God also came to those great prophets Elijah and Elisha.
Mary was visited by the angel Gabriel and the Holy Ghost
came upon her with the power of the highest when she
was alone and hid from the world. Then she received
Christ within her. The woman who first witnessed the joy
of Christ's resurrection was alone with Him at the sepulchre (John 20). It has always been that those who are in
retirement and secret converse with God are specially
blessed.

XI. Gracious Affections Intensify Spiritual Longings

Another great and distinguishing feature of gracious affections is that the more they are heightened the greater
will be the spiritual appetite and longing of soul for such
spiritual blessings to be increased. In contrast, false affections are satisfied with themselves.

The more a true saint loves God with a gracious love,
the more he desires to love Him.[2] His uneasiness concern-

---

[2]"Truly there is no work of Christ that is right, but it carries a soul to long for
more of it" (Shepard, *Parable of the Ten Virgins*, part 1, p. 136).

ing his lack of love for God will increase. The more he hates sin, the more he will want to hate it. He will regret that he still has so much remaining love for it. The more his heart is broken, the more he will want it to be broken further. The more he thirsts and longs after God and His holiness, the more he will long and breathe out his very soul in more longings after God. Like a kindled flame that rises higher, the more ardently it burns, the more it will continue to burn. Again, the babe at its mother's breast has his sharpest appetite when in the best of health. "As newborn babes desire the sincere milk of the Word, that you may grow thereby: if so be you have tasted that the Lord is gracious" (1 Peter 2:2, 3). This is a general principle that we find in many other Scriptures (see 2 Corinthians 1:22; Ephesians 1:14; 1 Corinthians 13:10, 11; Philippians 3:13-15).

The reasons for this are that the more people have holy affections, the more they will enjoy that spiritual taste of which I have spoken elsewhere. The more they perceive the excellence of God and relish the divine sweetness of holiness, the more grace they have and the more they see their need of grace. This increases their desire for more. Therefore, the cry of every true believer is: "Lord, I believe, help my unbelief" (Mark 9:24). The greater the spiritual discoveries and affections the true Christian has, the more he becomes an earnest supplicant for more grace and spiritual fruit.

We may cite four reasons to explain this principle of expansion. First of all, spiritual enjoyments are such that those who find them realize they are incomparably satisfying. Therefore they cannot be content with anything less. *Spiritual enjoyments are incomparable.*

Second, spiritual enjoyments satisfy the expectation of the appetite. The more they are anticipated, the more they are enjoyed. This cannot be found with worldly enjoyments; with them, there can only be disappointment. But spiritual enjoyments fully answer and satisfy all expectations. *Spiritual enjoyments are always better than we could anticipate.*

Spiritual enjoyments are lasting.

Third, unlike worldly enjoyments, the gratification and pleasure of spiritual enjoyments is permanent. Worldly enjoyments satiate, but when the appetite is glutted, the pleasure is over. Once the satisfaction is gone, the heart is empty and remains dissatisfied.

Spiritual enjoyments always satisfy.

Fourth, spiritual good always satisfies because there is always enough in it to satisfy the soul to whatever degree the soul is able to enjoy it. There is always room enough here for the soul to expand itself, until it becomes like an infinite ocean. If people are not satisfied, it is simply because they have not opened their mouths wide enough to receive it. Spiritual good is so satisfying that the more the soul tastes of it and knows its nature, the more it will desire, even when it is already satisfied.

The nature of spiritual affections is that the greater they become, the greater will be the appetite and longing for grace and holiness.

False joys are the opposite.

In contrast, false joys and religious affections have the opposite effect. The more they are aroused, the more they quench any longings for grace and holiness. So a person may think he is enriched and increased with goods. He may hardly be able to conceive of anything better than what he already has materially. He becomes smugly self-satisfied. This sometimes happens with people after their initial conversion. At first they did have intense affections that made them fully confident of their desire for God. Before their conversion they had been intent on seeking after God and crying earnestly for grace and striving by all means to attain it. But now they have become satisfied. They settle down, and no longer seek after God, which is the distinguishing character of the saints. They are not like those that Psalm 24:6 describes: "This is a generation of them that seek Him, that seek your face, O Jacob!" (cf. Psalm 69:6, 32; 70:4).

Spiritual self-satisfaction is self-defeating.

The Scriptures often represent the search, effort, and labor that occur in a Christian chiefly after his conversion. Yet his conversion is only the beginning of his work. From then on he has to stand, press forward, reach out, continue instant in prayer, and cry to God day and night. For the Lord "fills the hungry with good things, while the rich are sent away empty" (Luke 1:53).

There may be some pseudo-Christians who argue that they can stand this test. They claim they are dissatisfied with past achievements and want to press forward and desire more. But the truth is that their desires are not really desires after holiness for its own sake, or for the moral excellence and sweetness of God. They are only the means to obtain what they really long for: clear insight to help them have more satisfaction about themselves, or gratification in self-discovery, and in exalting themselves above other people.

These are very different from true spiritual desires after God. For the inward, burning desire that a saint has after holiness is as natural to the new creature as bodily heat is to the body. "My meat is to do the will of Him that sent me, and to finish His work" (John 4:34). We read in the Scriptures of the desires, longings, and thirsts of the saints for God's righteousness and His laws. The saints desire the sincere milk of the Word, not so much to testify to God's love for them, but rather that they will grow in holiness. As I have shown before, holiness is valued by a true spiritual taste. Grace is the godly man's treasure (Isaiah 33:6). Godliness is what he desires (1 Timothy 6:6). But the insights that a hypocrite longs for have no sanctifying influence. They are not really longings for a taste of God's love, nor are they longings to be in heaven, as are the longings of the true saints who seek after holy living.

I now come to the last distinguishing mark of holy affections that I shall mention.

IX
GRACIOUS AFFECTIONS ARE INTENSELY PRACTICAL

XII. GRACIOUS AFFECTIONS ARE THE DAILY PRACTICE OF CHRISTIAN MINISTRY

hey cause a Christian to be practical in the business of his daily life. Three things are implied by this. One, his behavior or practice in the world is wholly conformed to and directed by Christian principles. Two, he places holy living above everything else. This is his main preoccupation; he is devoted to it with the greatest diligence and earnestness. It can be said he makes his practice of true religion eminently his work and business. And three, he persists in it to the end of his life. He never takes a holiday from it, nor does he practice it only at certain times. It is the constant business of his life and he perseveres through all vicissitudes and under all the trials as long as he lives. The necessity of each of these traits in all true Christians is clearly and fully taught in the Word of God.

It may be noted first that all need to be obedient to this. "Every man that has this hope in him purifies himself, even as he is pure," "whoever abides in Him sins not," "he ..ho does righteousness is righteous, even as He is righteous" (1 John 3:3, etc.). "We know that whoever is born of God sins not, but he that is begotten of God keeps himself, and that wicked one touches him not" (1 John 5:18; cf. John 15:14). Naaman's hypocrisy was that while he seemed much affected with gratitude to God for healing his leprosy and although he pledged to serve Him, yet he asked to be excused of one thing. Herod feared John and heard him gladly, yet he was condemned for the one thing to which he would not assent, parting with his beloved Herodias. But if there is a right hand or eye which sins, then it must be dealt with. There can be no exceptions.

Christian obedience is total commitment.

It is also important to note that to be wholly obedient, one's obedience must involve sins of omission as well as sins of commission. If not there is the condemnation that our Lord gives in Matthew 25: "I was hungry, and you gave me no meat." It is not simply that we keep taboos and go no farther. It is necessary that we be serious, devout, humble, meek, forgiving, peaceful, respectful, benevolent, and so on.

True Christians are wholly earnest in their callings.

Second, in order to be true Christians, it is necessary that we pursue the business of religion and the service of God with great earnestness and diligence. All Christ's saints not only do good works, but they also are zealous of good works (Titus 2:14). No man can serve two masters at once. So we have to serve God with all our hearts, as Paul did, saying, "This one thing I do" (Philippians 3:13). If there is a fight to be fought, or a race to be won, then it must be done with utmost earnestness. Without this there is no way of traveling the narrow road that leads to life. Sloth is therefore as damning as open rebellion. The writer to the Hebrews says, "We desire that every one of you show the same diligence, to the full assurance of hope unto the end; that you are not slothful, but followers of them, who through faith and patience inherit the promises."

True Christians persevere wholeheartedly.

Every true Christian perseveres in this way of universal allegiance and diligent and earnest service to God. He does so through all kinds of trials that he may meet throughout his life. Many passages of Scripture clearly teach this. By trials I mean those things that occur to test us in our duty and faithfulness to God. Trials or temptations are of various kinds, such as those that make our way and duty difficult, or those that arouse our lusts and corrupt us. Or they are those that allure and entice us to sin. Some trials make our duty difficult to do. There are sufferings such as pain, ill will, contempt, reproach, loss of material possessions and comforts. But it is God's purpose in His providence to bring trials to us, in order to deepen our convictions and to test us.

True saints may be guilty of some degree and kind of backsliding, and they may even fall into sin. Nevertheless, they do not fall utterly away. They can never truly backslide as long as they continue in complete allegiance to Christ. Those who are truly converted are new men, new not only within but without, for they are sanctified throughout in body, soul, and spirit.

As I have said, gracious affections have their exercise and fruit in Christian practice. The reason they have such a tendency and effect has already been discussed: Gracious affections come from those operations and influences which are truly spiritual, and partake of the divine nature. Christ lives in the heart and the Holy Spirit dwells there in union with the faculties of the soul as an internal, vital principle that exerts God's own proper nature. This is why true grace has such active power and efficacy. If God dwells in the heart and is vitally united to it, He will show that He is God by the efficacy of His operation. For Christ is not dead but alive. And so when Christ is savingly in a heart, He will live and exert Himself according to the power of the endless life He received at His resurrection. Thus every saint is a subject of the benefit of Christ's sufferings and is made to know and experience the power of His resurrection. It is all power and all action "in demonstration of the Spirit and of power" (1 Corinthians 2:4). "Our gospel came not unto you in word only, but also in power, and in the Holy Ghost" (1 Thessalonians 1:5; cf. 1 Corinthians 4:20; 2 Corinthians 10:5).

Christ's presence in us is always fruitful.

Thus we have evidence that godliness is effective in its practice. The Apostle thus preached about the power of

Godliness is powerful.

godliness (2 Timothy 3:5). This power is seen in the practical exercise of holy affections: conquering the world, overcoming the lusts and corruptions of men, and carrying men forward in the way of holiness despite temptations, difficulty, and opposition.

Gracious affections have efficacy, because of the transcendent excellence of divine things. These are intrinsic in themselves, and bear no conceived relation to self or to self-interest. It is this that causes men to be holy in all their practice. In turn this helps them to persevere all the time. For the nature of religion is invariably always the same, at all times, and through all changes. It never alters in any respect.

The foundation of all holy affections is in moral excellence and the beauty of holiness. There is a love of holiness for its own sake that inclines people to practice holiness. Holiness is thus the main business that excites, draws, and governs all gracious affections. No wonder then that all such affections tend to holiness, for men will be united to and possessed by that which they love and desire. And what has been observed of the divine teaching and leading of the Spirit of God in gracious affections will show a tendency toward a universal, holy practice. The Holy Spirit gives the soul a natural relish for the sweetness of what is holy and for everything that is holy as it comes into view. He also intensifies a dislike and disgust of everything that is unholy.

Spiritual knowledge is also practical. The same thing may be observed in the nature of spiritual knowledge, which is the foundation of all holy affection. Its senses and view of the excellence of divine things is supreme and transcendent. These things appear to be worthy above all others that may be chosen and adhered to. By the sight of the transcendent glory of Christ, true Christians see Him as worthy to be followed, so they are powerfully drawn after Him. Seeing Him worthy, they are prepared to forsake all for Him. The sight of such superlative loveliness thoroughly disposes them to be subject to Him. They are prepared to labor with all earnestness and activity in His service and are willing to go through all difficulties for His sake. This discovery makes them constant in their loyalty to Him. It makes a deep impression on their minds so that they can never forget Him. They will follow Him wherever He goes; anyone's attempt to seduce them from Him will be vain.

Another reason there is this practical tendency and consequence of gracious affections is that those who have them are thoroughly convicted of the judgment, reality, and certainty of divine things. Those who are not convinced there is any reality in the things of religion will never labor and work with an all-prevailing earnestness and perseverance through all the difficulties, self-denials, and sufferings. But those who are convinced of the certain truth of these things will be governed by them in their practice. To them the realities revealed in the Word of God are so great and so infinitely more important than anything else, that if a person believes in them it is inconsistent with human nature that he should not be influenced by them in practice.

Spiritual convictions also promote practice.

Another reason for the practical consequences of holy affections is the change of nature that accompanies such affections. Without such a change man's actions would not be thoroughly changed. And until the tree is made good, the fruit will not be good. Men do not gather grapes from thorns, nor figs from thistles. But as long as corrupt nature is not dead, the principle of corruption is alive in him and therefore it is vain to expect it to be controlled. It is not natural for a natural man to deny his lust and live a strictly religious life. But when the old nature is dead and a new and heavenly nature replaces it, then it may well be expected that men will walk in newness of life, continuing to do so until the end of their days.

Holy affections change lives practically.

This practical exercise and effect of holy affections may also be partly seen by the associated spirit of humility. Much of the spirit of obedience consists of humility. A proud spirit is a rebellious spirit, but a humble spirit is docile, subject, and obedient. We see that the

Then humility will also be practiced.

strong-willed servant is not likely to be submissive and obedient to his master's word. The opposite is true with the servant of a humble spirit. We have already spoken of the lamblike, dovelike spirit which accompanies all gracious affections, as the Apostle observes in Romans 13:8-10 and Galatians 5:14. Christian practice consists very much then in the external practice of Christianity.

We have also seen that gracious affections are associated with obedience and a tender spirit that is sensitive to the presence of moral evil. It dreads all the appearance of evil.

Gracious affections are always constant.

A major reason Christian practice stems from gracious affections is the pervasive, constant, and persevering outflow of the affections themselves. They are always consistent and so have a winsome symmetry and balance. We see that in holy affections there is earnestness, action, commitment, perseverance, and holy practice because of the spiritual appetite and longing for further achievements which always are associated with true affections. These never decay, but increase as the affections increase.

Thus we see that the tendency of holy affections to be expressed in Christian practice occurs as a result of each of the characteristics of holy affections that we have addressed.

Scripture illustrates how practical gracious affections are.

This is further illustrated and confirmed by the Holy Scriptures' emphasis to Christians to make a full choice of God as our only Lord and to forsake all for Him. Importance is thus placed on the full determination to do the will of God in Christ, whatever the cost. It is described as our "heart's closure" to comply in absolute trust in Jesus Christ. Such faith is embraced in spite of all difficulties, since we are prepared to give ourselves wholly to Him. This is done unreservedly in the great duty of self-denial for Christ.[1]

---

[1]Matthew 4:18-22; 5:29, 30; 6:24; 8:19-22; 10:37-39; 13:44-46; 16:24-26; 18:8, 9; 19:21, 27-29; Luke 5:27, 28; 10:42; 12:33, 34; 14:16-20, 25-33; 16:13; Acts 4:34, 35; 5:1-11; Romans 6:3-8; Galatians 2:20; 6:14; Philippians 3:7.

Having a heart to forsake all for Christ surely means then that we are prepared actually to forsake all for Him. It is having a self-denying heart for Christ's sake. This tends to be a denial of ourselves whenever Christ and our self-interest are in competition. To give up ourselves, unreservedly, leads to a general subjection to His will and purpose. Our heart's total commitment is to Jesus with all that that means and in spite of all its difficulties. This tends to promote action and deeds, in patience and in perseverance.

This tendency of grace in the heart to practice holiness is specific and natural. True grace is not inactive. Indeed, there is nothing in heaven and on earth that has a more active nature, for it is life itself. And it is the most active kind of life, for it is spiritual and divine life. It can never be barren, for its nature has a greater tendency to bear fruit than anything else. Godliness in the heart has as direct a relationship to practice as a fountain has to a stream, or the luminous nature of the sun has to the sunbeams that are sent forth, or as life has to breathing, or the beating of the pulse, or any other vital act. The very nature and notion of grace is that it is a principle of holy action and practice.

Nothing is more practical than grace in the heart.

Regeneration, which is that work of God in which grace is infused, has a direct relationship to practice; indeed, it is the very purpose of it. All this is calculated and designed for the mighty and manifold change that is wrought in the world. "For we are His workmanship, created in Christ Jesus to good works" (Ephesians 2:10). It is the very purpose of Christ's redemption, "Who gave Himself for us, that He might redeem us from all iniquity and purify unto Himself a peculiar people, zealous of good works" (Titus 2:14). See also Ephesians 1:4; 2:10; Matthew 3:10; 13:8, 23, 30, 38; 21:19, 33, 34; Luke 13:6; John 15:1, 2, 4-6, 8; 1 Corinthians 3:9; Hebrews 6:7, 8; Isaiah 5:1-8; Song of Solomon 8:11, 12; Isaiah 27:2, 3.[2]

---

[2]"To profess to know much is easy; but to bring your affections into subjection, to wrestle with lusts, to cross your wills and yourselves, upon every occasion, this is hard" (Dr. John Preston, *In the Church's Carriage*, pp. 101-102).

Therefore everything in the true Christian is calculated to this end. This fruit of holy practice is a direct tendency that belongs to grace in every Christian experience.

Only true saints can be so practical.

It may also be noted that this fruit of Christian practice which is always found in true saints is only found in them alone. None but true saints can live such an obedient life, or be so devoted to their duty and given to the business of being real Christians. All unsanctified people are workers of iniquity and grow the lusts of their fathers. "Every tree is known by his own fruit" (Luke 6:44).

The Scripture plainly teaches that practice is the best evidence of the sincerity or profession of Christians. Our reason teaches the same thing. It is reasonable to believe that men's deeds are a better and more faithful interpreter of their minds than are their mere words. This is common sense. All mankind, in all ages, has taught this as a criterion by which to judge the hearts of men. And so the best evidence of friendship toward Christ, for example, is in the words of John 14:21: "He that has My commandments and keeps them, he it is that loves Me." It is practice then that makes profession credible. But further things may be observed so that this can be rightly understood.

Faith practiced is faith professed.

In the first place, note that when Scripture speaks of Christian practice as the best evidence before others for the sincerity and truth of grace, this does not exclude a profession of Christianity. The rules that we have mentioned above were rules given to the followers of Christ, to guide them in assessing professing Christians. By these they can judge the truth of the pretenses and the sincerity of their profession of faith. They are not therefore rules for pagans and those that make no pretense of being Christians.

"Show me your faith without your works, and I will show you my faith by my works" (James 2:18). It is evident here that both kinds of person, offering diverse evidences of their faith, are professors of faith. Profession is not the main piece of evidence, nor does it distinguish it, yet it is required and necessary. If anyone plainly says that he is

not a Christian and does not believe that Jesus is the Son
of God, then these rules of Christ do not apply to him.

Then when is a man said to profess Christianity? What
really is a profession of Christianity? There are two aspects
to the answer.

The first aspect is that anyone who makes a profession
of Christianity must have the essence of it. He must be
able to declare that he has the essential reality. If we pick
and choose some part of Christianity, leaving out what is
essential to it, then we cannot say that we are making a
real profession of it. For example, in order to make a profession of Christianity we must profess that we believe
that Jesus is the Messiah. For this is a belief that is vital to
it. It is also essential to believe that we must repent of our
sins or we will be exposed to the wrath of God. Indeed, we
must believe all the main doctrines of the gospel. We must
be convicted of the need of repentance. We must embrace
Christ and rely upon Him as our Savior with all our hearts,
and joyfully dwell on the gospel of Christ.

*To profess truly
is to know
essentially.*

The second aspect is that the profession of what belongs to Christian faith and how it is related to Christian
practice implies an understanding of the consequences of
such a profession. I am not saying that we have to give an
account of our experiences. But it does mean that what we
profess, we have to experience actually for ourselves. So
for us to profess solemnly full conviction of our own utter
sinfulness, misery, and helplessness, of our just desert of
God's utter rejection and eternal wrath, as well as the
utter insufficiency of our own righteousness, does mean
that we have actually experienced what we are talking
about. But unless we depend entirely on the Lord Jesus
Christ and His satisfaction of sin, then our profession
really means nothing at all. Merely to profess Christianity, as either a habit or as a cultural feature, is to falsify the
very character of the faith required of us.

*To profess truly
is to know the
consequences.*

This does not mean that we have to make a clear account of the way we were first converted. But it does mean
that we have to be able to demonstrate that we have

experienced what we are talking about. It is unscriptural to insist that we give a particular account of the distinct method and steps of how the Spirit of God has sensibly dealt with us, in order to bring us to salvation.

To profess truly means to live a holy life.

We must also understand what we mean by Christian practice. It is not just saying that a professor of Christianity is what is commonly called an honest, or an upright man. This does not necessarily indicate any work or any labor of love that is expressed in the name of Christ such as persuaded the Apostle of the sincerity of the professing Hebrews (Hebrews 6:9, 10). There must also be some strong evidence of holiness in a man's visible behavior. Such a life must appear to be the life of the servants of God. We must show that we follow the example of Jesus Christ. We must rise to a considerable measure to those marvelous rules described in the fifth, sixth, and seventh chapters of Matthew, the twelfth chapter of Romans, as well as many other parts of the New Testament. We must demonstrate that we walk as Christians, everywhere and all the time. We must show clear evidence of a spirit of self-denial and a willingness to suffer for Christ and on behalf of our brethren.

We should also recognize that there are no outward evidences or appearances of the infallible proofs of grace. Such evidences, we have already noted, are only the best that a natural man can have. But external appearances and imitations of grace are not enough to ensure that a person is truly a child of God.

To profess truly is to have a good conscience.

Having considered Christian practice as the best evidence of the sincerity of its professors before others, I now proceed to another observation. This is that the Scriptures also speak of Christians having a sure and distinguishing evidence of grace in their own consciences. This is very plain in 1 John 2:3: "Hereby we know that we know Him, if we keep His commandments." Our consciences are assured by the testimony of good deeds. "My little children, let us not love in word, neither in tongue, but in deed and in truth. And hereby we know that we are

of the truth, and shall assure our hearts before Him"
(1 John 3:18, 19). Likewise, the Apostle in Hebrews 6:9
speaks of the work and labor of love that these Hebrew
Christians had demonstrated (cf. Galatians 6:4; Psalm
119:6; Matthew 7:19, 20). We have also the solemn
words of our Lord: "Not everyone that says to me, 'Lord,
Lord,' shall enter the Kingdom of Heaven; but he that
does the will of My Father, which is in heaven. Many will
say to Me in that day, 'Lord, Lord.' Then I will profess to
them, I never knew you, depart from Me you that work iniquity."

But for greater clarity on this matter, let me first show
how Christian practice is considered in the Scriptures to
be a sure sign to our own consciences that we are real
Christians. Second, we will show that this is the chief evidence that a man can have of his own sincere godliness.

First of all then, note that the Scriptures, when speaking of good works, or good fruit, or keeping Christ's commandments, do not describe merely something that is outward. They deal also with the understanding or will.
When obedience and fruit are spoken of, they do not refer
only to the acts of the body, but also to those of the soul.
They refer therefore to every kind of inward exercise of
grace. But beyond these inward acts of obedience, there is
also implied the decision of the will to be obedient.

*Christian practice
is inward as well
as outward.*

In order to understand more clearly what I am meaning, let us note that there are two kinds of exercise of
grace. First, there are immanent acts, or exercises of grace
within the soul that have no outward evidence of their
practice. Such are what the saints often have in contemplation when the exercise is within the heart alone.

The second kind of act of grace is more practical or effective exercises. They are exertions of grace in response
to the command of the will and are directed in outward actions. So when a saint gives a cup of cold water, he is exercising the grace of charity. Or when he voluntarily en-
dures persecution, in the course of duty, he is exercising
supreme love to Christ. In these instances, the exercise of

grace produces the effect of some outward action in practical and productive ways. Such is properly the exercise of grace in the act of the will.

Dr. Doddridge has observed that the determinations of the will are indeed our very actions, so far as they are properly ours.[3] Such effective exercises of grace are experienced to an high degree by martyrs. But all true saints live a life of such devotion. This is the obedience and fruit that God looks for as He looks into the soul. "For the Lord sees not as man sees, for He looks upon the heart."

Thus when obedience, good works, and good fruit are taken as sure evidence of the principle of grace, these remain external in the view of others. But when their practice is also evidence of the reality of Christianity to our own consciences, then its practice is visible internally to our own consciences also. Then we see that it is not merely the outward, bodily efforts but also the internal exertion of the soul which directs and commands those actions. This is the intent of Scripture.

Christian practice is like building upon a rock.

At the conclusion of the Sermon on the Mount, Christ speaks of the doing or practicing of these sayings of His as a clear sign of who are true disciples. He likens the true saint to a man that built his house upon the rock, in contrast to one who built it upon the sands. In this illustration He regards not only the outward behavior, but the inward exercise of the mind in that behavior. So Christ says: "He that has My commandments, and keeps them, he it is that loves Me" (John 14:21; cf. 1 John 2:3, 7-11).

Thus we see in Scripture that much evidence of what is sincere depends on what is inward. At the same time, what is outward is also included and needed as a practical connection with the exercise of grace in the world, directing and controlling the actions of the body. There has to be consistency between what is outward and what is inward.

---

[3]Phillip Doddridge, "The Scripture Doctrine of Salvation," *Practical Discourses on Regeneration*, Philadelphia, 1796).

X

THE AFFECTIONS ARE THE CHIEF EVIDENCE OF A SAVING SINCERITY IN TRUE RELIGION

hristian practice is much more to be preferred as evidence of salvation than sudden conversion, mystical enlightenment, or the mere experience of emotional comfort that begins and ends with contemplation.[1] The evidence for this will appear in the six following arguments.

Argument 1

Reason plainly demonstrates that the proper test of what man really prefers is to see what he actually cleaves to and practices when given a choice. Sincerity of religion has already been observed to consist in setting God highest in the heart, in choosing Him above everything else, and in giving up everything for Christ. But a man's actions are the proper test of his heart. If, for example, when God and other things, whether worldly interests or pleasures,

True religion sets God above all else.

---

[1] "Look at John, Christ's beloved disciple and bosom companion! He had been assured that he knew Him that is true, and he knew that he knew Him" (1 John 2:3). But how did he know that? He might be deceived, since it is amazing what a melancholic imagination will do and the effects it will have. As honest men are reputed to have weak brains and never see the depths of the secret of God, what then is John's ultimate evidence? "Because we keep His commandments." (Shepard, *Parable of the Ten Virgins*, part 1, p. 131.).

179

are in competition with each other, a man's behavior will be tested by what he actually prefers and cleaves to, and what he forsakes. Sincerity consists then in forsaking all for Christ in the heart, and in forsaking all for Christ when called on. Doing this is the test. So godliness consists not merely in having a heart intent on doing the will of God, but having a heart that actually does it. In Deuteronomy 5:27-29 the Israelites had a heart intending to keep God's commandments. But God shows that this was very far from what He desired because they did not actually keep them.

It is absurd then to pretend to have a good heart while living a wicked life. For the plain fact of experience cannot then be disputed. "Be not deceived; God is not mocked; for whatsoever a man sows, that shall he also reap" (Galatians 6:7). Such pretense not actually practiced is often described in Scripture with the word *mock.* So Delilah says to Samson, "Behold, you have mocked me, and told me lies" (Judges 16:10, 13). Men may be so deceived, but the great Judge, whose eyes are as a flame of fire, will not be mocked nor misled by any pretenses. "There is no darkness, nor shadow of death, where the workers of iniquity may hide themselves" (Job 34:22).

Argument 2

True religion will be tested.

In Scripture the truth of real faith is often tested by what is difficult to overcome. Trials or temptations[2] are the vital proofs by which to determine truly whether men have the right disposition of heart to cleave to God or not. "And you shall remember all the way which the LORD your God led you these forty years in the wilderness, to humble you, to prove you, whether you would keep His commandments or not" (Deuteronomy 8:2; cf. Joshua 2:21, 22; Judges 3:1, 4; Exodus 16:4).

These difficulties of faith are called temptations or trials in Scripture to test men's faith. "My brothers, count

---

[2] 2 Corinthians 8:2; Hebrews 11:36; 1 Peter 1:7; 4:12, among many others.

it all joy when you fall into diverse temptations; knowing this, that the trying of your faith works patience" (James 1:2, 3). "Now for a season you are in heaviness, through manifold temptations; that the trial of your faith being much more precious than gold" (1 Peter 1:6, 7). Likewise, the Apostle Paul speaks of giving to the poor as proof of the sincerity of the love of Christians (2 Corinthians 8:8). Such tests are often illustrated by the refining of gold and silver (Psalm 66:10, 11; Zechariah 13:9; Revelation 3:17, 18).

When God is said to have proved Israel by the difficulties that they met within the wilderness and from their enemies in Canaan, it was in order to know what was in their hearts, whether they would keep His commandments or not. Likewise when God tempted Abraham with that difficult command of offering up his son, He said to him: "Now I know that you fear God, seeing you have not withheld your son, your only son, from me." Christ used this same test with the rich young man in Matthew 19:16.

Such trials are not for God's benefit, but for our own. To try ourselves in these ways is the surest way that we can discern a correct judgment upon ourselves. If we want to know whether a building will stand strong or not, we look at it when the wind is blowing hard. Similarly, we can list the reality of a man's Christian practice when he is under the trials of God's providence.

Argument 3

Such holy practice, in the sense in which we have explained, is the best kind of evidence of the reality of grace in the Christian's conscience. The Apostle James says concerning it: "See how faith wrought with his works and by works faith was perfect" (James 2:22), or as the word in the original indicates "was completed." So the love of God is said to be finished or completed in keeping His commandments. "He that says, I know Him, and keeps not His commandments, is a liar and the truth is not in him: but whoso keeps His word, in him truly is the perfect love of God" (1 John 2:4, 5).

True religion matures by practice.

182 The Distinguishing Signs of Holy Affections

Grace or the love of God is said to be perfected in holy practice just as a tree is made perfect in the fruit that it bears. It is not perfected when the seed is merely planted in the ground or even when it brings forth leaves, or even when it blossoms. It is only when it brings forth good and ripe fruit that it is perfected. For then it has reached its desired end. Such then is grace in its practical exercises.

Argument 4

The real test of true religion is its practice.

Scripture insists on the importance of holy practice as the principal evidence for judging both our own sincerity and that of others. "By this you shall know that you know God: by this is manifest the children of God, and the children of the devil: he that has this, builds on a good foundation; he that has it not, builds on the sand; hereby we shall assure our hearts." Of all the evidences of true godliness, none is more often specified than of having love one to another. "We know that we have passed from death unto life, because we love the brethren" (1 John 3:14; cf. Romans 13:8, 10; Galatians 5:14; Matthew 22:39, 40).

Argument 5

Grace is evident in practice.

Christian practice is also plainly spoken of in the Word of God as the main evidence of the truth of grace, not only for others but for our own consciences. It is represented as the main evidence for oneself. "He that has My commandments, and keeps them, he it is that loves Me" (John 14). The repetition of this emphasis is remarkable, for He says in verse 15, "If you love Me, keep My commandments"; verse 23, "If a man loves Me, he will keep My words"; and verse 24, "He that loves Me not, keeps not My sayings." In the next chapter He repeats the same emphasis over and over again (John 15:2, 8, 14). We have the same emphasis in 1 John.

Argument 6

This great evidence of holy practice will be used before the judgment seat of God. In the future judgment there will be an open trial of professors, and evidences will be used to judge them. Such a declarative judgment will reveal the righteousness of God's judgment to men's own consciences and to the world. Therefore the Day of Judgment is called "the Day of the Revelation of the Righteous Judgment of God" (Romans 2:5; cf. Matthew 18:31; 20:8-15; 22:11-13; 25:19-30; Luke 19:15-23). The Scriptures abundantly teach us that the Judge's major evidence will be men's works or practice here in this world (Revelation 20:12; 2 Corinthians 5:10; and many other references). "For God will bring every work into judgment, with every secret thing, whether it be good, or whether it be evil" (Ecclesiastes 12:14).

In the Day of Judgment practice will be the evidence.

From this we can undoubtedly infer that men's works, taken in the sense it has been explained, are the chief evidence by which they ought to try themselves now. Our supreme Judge will make full use of them to judge us when we come to stand before Him, if in the meantime we have not made use of them to judge ourselves.[3] If it had not been revealed in this way and by what evidence the Judge would proceed with us, it would be natural for someone to ask, "How could I know what God would look for and insist upon in that last and decisive judgment?" But since God has so plainly and abundantly revealed what this evidence will be, surely it is sensible and of the greatest importance to test ourselves by it now.

Christian practice then is the evidence above all other evidence that confirms and crowns a proof of godliness. It is also proper proof of the true and saving knowledge of God: "Hereby do we know that we know Him, that we

Practice proves godliness.

---

[3]"That which God makes a rule in His own judgment is that by which He will judge every man, is a sure rule for every man to judge himself by. Now by our obedience and works He judges us. He will give to every man according to his works" (Preston, *Church's Carriage*, p. 99).

keep His commandments." For if we know God, but glorify Him not as God, then our knowledge will only condemn us and not save us (Romans 1:21). "If you know these things, happy are you if you do them" (John 13:17).

Practice is evidence of repentance.
Holy practice is the proper evidence of repentance. When the Jews professed repentance, confessing their sins to John in the Baptism of Repentance, he directed them to the right way: "Bring forth fruits meet for repentance" (Matthew 3:8).

Practice is evidence of saving faith.
Holy practice is the proper evidence of a saving faith, as seen in the example the Apostle James gives of Abraham (James 2:21-24). Practice is the best evidence of a saving belief in the truth. "I rejoiced greatly when the brethren came and testified of the truth, that it is in you, even as you walk in the truth" (3 John 3).

Practice is evidence of Christ's presence.
Holy practice is the best evidence of a true coming to Christ and an acceptance of Him. Indeed, Christ promises us eternal life on the condition that we come to Him. Practice is also the true evidence of trusting in Christ for our salvation. Such a commitment is a practical reality of dependence. "For the which cause I also suffer these things; nevertheless I am not ashamed, for I know whom I have believed, and I am persuaded that He is able to keep that which I have committed unto Him against that day" (2 Timothy 1:12).

Practice is evidence of divine love.
Holy practice is also the true evidence of a gracious love both to God and men. It is also the evidence of humility and of a fear of God. It is evidence of true gratitude: "What shall I render to the LORD for all His benefits toward me?" (Psalm 116:12). The Psalmist also indicates, "Whoso offers praise, glorifies Me: and to him that orders his conversation aright, will I show the salvation of God" (Psalm 50:23). Again, practice is real evidence of gracious desires and longings, of a gracious hope, of doing the will of God in holy love, of Christian fortitude, and of the truth of grace.

Before I conclude this discourse, let me briefly answer two objections that question Christian practice as the paramount evidence of saving grace.

The first objection is that a professing Christian's inward, spiritual experiences should be the main evidence of true grace. Does not this holy practice of the mind govern and direct its bodily expressions? Indeed, these inward exercises are by no means the least aspect of Christian experience since outward behavior is intimately connected with them. But to speak of Christian experience and practice as two different things is to make an unreasonable distinction. Indeed, all Christian experience is not properly called practice, but all Christian practice is experienced. To distinguish them is unscriptural. Jeremiah asks, "Did not your father eat and drink, and do justice and judgment? He judged the cause of the poor and the needy . . . was not this to know Me, says the Lord?" (Jeremiah 22:15, 16). Our inward knowledge of God will dominate our religious experience, or holy practice. Many Scriptures could be cited to illustrate this; for example, 1 John 5:3; 2 John 6; Psalm 34:11, and in much of Psalm 119, and elsewhere.

There is a type of externalized religious practice with no inward experience, which is of no account to God. It is good for nothing. And there is also experience without any practice, and which has no Christian behavior. This is worse than nothing. For whenever a person finds within himself a heart to relate to God as God and he is tested, he will always find his disposition effective in the practical experience of it. If then religion consists largely of holy affection, true religion is most distinguished in the practical exercise of affection. Friendship between earthly friends consists of much affection, but when such strong bonds of affection take them through great difficulties, in this they have the proof of true friendship.

When theologians say that there are no sure evidences of grace without the deeds of grace, they are saying what we see in everyday experience. Once a man has seen his neighbor, he has proof of his existence. But by seeing him daily and talking frequently with him in various

Is inward experience not more important than outward appearance?

circumstances, the evidence is established. For example, the disciples, when they first saw Christ after His resurrection, had good evidence that He was alive. But after conversing with Him for forty days, and seeing many infallible proofs of His identity, they had still greater proof.[4] Likewise the witness or seal of the Spirit is seen in the effect of the Spirit of God upon the heart. As grace is implanted and exercised, so its experience grows. This indwelling presence of the Holy Spirit is the greatest evidence of our adoption as the children of God.

Is it legalism to emphasize need of outward practice?

It may also be objected that the insistence upon Christian practice as the chief evidence of the reality of grace is a legal doctrine. To make practice so important only exalts self-effort, leaving people to make too much of their own actions to the loss of the glory of free grace. How is this consistent with the great gospel doctrine of justification by faith alone?

This objection is quite unreasonable. How can holy practice as a sign of His grace be inconsistent with the freeness of God's grace? It would be unreasonable to barter our works as the price of God's favor. But to say their exercise is proof of the gift of grace is not inconsistent. The unworthiness of man to do anything righteous is what is important to emphasize. This is the Scripture's meaning of justification without works. We are justified only by the righteousness of Christ and not by our own righteousness. When works are opposed to faith in this matter, we are truly said to be justified by faith and not by works. But this is no argument against saying that grace will be expressed in holy practice. For surely it is inconsistent with the free gift of gospel grace that a title to salvation should be given

---

[4]"The more these visible exercises of grace are renewed, the more certain you will be. The more frequently these actions are renewed, the more abiding and confirmed your assurance will become. A man that has been assured of such visible exercises of grace may quickly doubt whether he is mistaken. But when these practices are renewed again and again, he grows more settled and established about his condition . . . the more men's grace is multiplied, the more their peace is multiplied: 'Grace and peace be multiplied unto you, through the knowledge of God, and Jesus our Lord'" (2 Peter 1:2). (Stoddard, *Way to Know Sincerity and Hypocrisy*, pp. 142, 143.

to men unless the benefits of Christ be expressed in a renewed, sanctified, and heavenly heart that loves God and is like God because it has the experience of joy in the Holy Ghost. To make light of works because we are not justified by works is the same as to make light of all true religion, all grace and holiness, and all gracious experience.

It is greatly to the detriment of true religion for people to make light of works and emphasize little those things which the Scripture demonstrates as most important. To assume this notion emphasizes legality and the old covenant is foolish. In vain we may look for better evidence of godliness than what the Scriptures give and most frequently insist upon. As Agur says: "Every word of God is pure; He is a shield to them that put their trust in Him: Do not add unto His words, lest He reprove you and you be found a liar" (Proverbs 30:5, 6). We cannot trust our own discernment of the hearts of men. We see little of the reality of the soul and the depths of man's heart. Personal affections may be moved without any supernatural influence. They are so buried and secretive and influenced in so many ways that they are not to be trusted.

Instead we must closely follow the clue which God has given us in His Word. God knows why He insists on some things and sets them forth for us to try ourselves by rather than by other means. Perhaps He knows what things are less perplexing and less liable to deceive. He best knows our own nature. He knows the nature and manner of His own operations. He best knows the way of our safety. He knows what allowances to make for the differing states of His church and the differing tempers of each person. Therefore it is wise for us not to take His work out of His own hands, and to follow Him in the way that He has directed us.

No wonder we get bewildered, confounded, and deluded if we do otherwise. However, if we get into the habit of looking chiefly at those things which Christ, His apostles, and prophets have emphasized and insisted upon, and so judge ourselves and others by the practical exercises and effects of grace while not neglecting other

Practical Christianity is God's purpose for us.

things, then the result will be good and blessed. It will lead to the conviction of misguided hypocrites and prevent the delusion of those only half-committed to the straight and narrow way which leads to life. It will help to deliver us from innumerable perplexities and from various inconsistent schemes that abound in experience. It will keep professors of faith from neglecting the strictness of life, and it will promote earnestness and commitment in their Christian walk.

True Christians should encourage each other in practical Christianity.

We shall then see a dynamic faith within our own generation. Christians who are intimate friends will then begin to talk together of their experiences and comforts in a way that is better becoming Christian humility and modesty and more to each other's advantage. Their tongues will not run before them, but rather behind their hands and feet, after the prudent example of the blessed Apostle (2 Corinthians 12:6). Thus a great door will be shut against the devil. Many of the major stumbling blocks against experiential and powerful faith will be removed.

Practical Christianity will lessen skepticism.

True religion will then be declared and revealed in such a way that men will become convinced that there is reality in religion, instead of becoming hardened spectators, skeptical or atheistic. This will challenge them and win them by convincing their consciences of the importance and excellency of true religion. Thus the light of such witness will so shine before men, that others seeing their good works will glorify their Father, who is in heaven.

Scripture Index

189

Subject Index

STUDY GUIDE FOR GROUP DISCUSSION

For those Christians who are perplexed today about religious revivals this treatise of Jonathan Edwards is a crucial study. Edwards had a revival in his own parish in 1734-1735, followed by "The Great Awakening" throughout New England, which in turn influenced John Wesley as well as Scottish church leaders. Edwards stood in the midst of the first worldwide revival movement of the eighteenth century, writing about it first in *A Faithful Narrative of the Surprising Works of God in the Conversion of Many Hundred Souls* (1737), and then in an apologetic, *The Distinguishing Marks of a Work of the Spirit of God* (1741), and with the end of the Awakening, *Some Thoughts Concerning the Present Revival of Religion in New England* (1742). Much had happened in the meanwhile: not only was the youth of his church, as well as others, remarkably blessed, but he himself went through a period of deep contrition, and his wife three years of ecstatic joy and inner blessing, followed by the campaigns of Whitefield and other preachers. Edwards never ceased to believe in the evidence of the Holy Spirit's work being present in these events, but he questioned more and more the physical signs: faintings, fallings, weeping, shouting, trances, and convulsions. There was even rivalry among congregations as to the most dramatic effects made, and even Whitefield was biased toward these "bodily effects" about which Edwards expressed his misgivings so strongly in 1740. The relationship between them was never the same again. Edwards' sermons in 1742-1743 were directed to these issues, which he published as *A Treatise Concerning Relig-*

ious Affections in 1746. It is a study profoundly relevant to our own times of confusion over such charismatic issues as "signs and wonders," the "Toronto blessings," and other revival movements.

PART ONE
THE NATURE AND IMPORTANCE OF THE AFFECTIONS

How Jonathan Edwards Exemplified True Spiritual Renewal (pp. 3-5)

There was spiritual progression in Edwards' life. No single experience was enough, nor normative, for others that followed: the Scriptures, creation, the sense of God's glory, then the beauty of Christ's redemption, all gave texture to his rich and joyous experiences of the Christian life.

1. What have been our experiences of spiritual stagnation or of stages of growth?
2. For Edwards, his experiences were of the excellency of God, kindling profound ardour, desire, and joy within his heart. But it was all grounded in Scripture, as his delight was to meditate upon 1 Timothy 1:17, the text of this classic. What Scripture passage fills us with similar delight in God?
3. Edwards' spiritual experiences were consistent with a series of awakenings in his life, as well as with growing interests he deliberately cultivated. 1 Peter 1:8-9 first became a challenge to him as a youth, and then continued to preoccupy him in the years ahead. Do we also share a similar sequence of spiritual events, or have yours been only in a congregational setting?
4. Edwards uses his favorite text to point out that trials and sufferings form the context of such spiritual awakenings. For suffering purifies faith, and the contrast between outward suffering and inward joy can be experienced together. Does this help us to discern the true from false spiritual emotionality?

"True Religion Lies Much in the Affections" (pp. 5-11)

1. One way Edwards discovered this was in the spiritual changes in his wife between 1741 and 1746. Before, she had

been rather judgmental, given to depression, and too dependent upon her husband for her own spiritual life. Then
over a period of sixteen days in January 1742, the Spirit of
God filled her in such a marvelous way that she developed
"a holy indifference" about the opinion of others, accompanied by exalted worship of Christ and a tremendous joy
within her that lasted for several years. Edwards now sought
to have the same experiences within himself. Has this happened similarly in your family?

2. In spite of his own intellectual bent as a great mind, Edwards
realized that love is a strong inclination of the will to be af-
fective. Confronted by a rationalism that devalued the emotions and exalted reason, he saw that this needed correction
by acknowledging our affectional being. Yet he also was confronted by a strong antinomianism that Christian experience
be exalting in private emotionalism. Discuss how we, too,
face both a false objectivism and a false subjectivism in reaction to each of these views in the churches today. The disposition of grace balances both tendencies, helping us have
an objective view of the beauty of God's holiness, as well as
our response to His love given to us in Christ. Discuss how
we still need to maintain this balance of "gracious affections" in our Christian life.

3. Passions and affections are not the same. How does Edwards
help us to distinguish them, and how important is it to do
so?

4. He said, "They who have but little religious affections, have
certainly but little religion. And they who condemn others
for their religious affections, and have none themselves,
have no religion." Do you agree with Edwards?

The Bible and Its Saints Emphasize the Affections (pp. 11-28)

1. "The Scriptures place much of religion in godly fear." Has
"the fear of the Lord" been a significant element in your own
spiritual growth?

2. Hope is also often intertwined with fear (Psalm 31:24; 33:18;
97:11; Romans 8:2; 1 Thessalonians 5:8; Hebrews 6:19; 1 Pe-

ter 1:3). How does such "hope" differ from mere optimism in these Scriptures?

3. Holy desire of God is also much evidenced (Isaiah 26:8; Psalm 27:4; 42:12; 84:12; Matthew 5:6). When are our desires for God inhibited?

4. The Pauline salutation of "love, joy, peace" may well summarize the positive affections of the life given to God. How are they related in our own experience of the Christian life? What else has struck you in this summary of Edwards' survey of biblical expressions and experiences of affections?

PART TWO
FALSE SIGNS OF SPIRITUAL LIFE AND ACTION WITHIN US

Ways in Which Affections/Emotions May Be Falsely Interpreted (pp. 33-44)

1. A fervent, intense spirit is no sign in itself of true affection for God. Yet we are to love God superlatively (Deuteronomy 6:5), be joyful exceedingly (Psalm 68:3), hate sin vehemently (Psalm 139:21-22). So how do we discern about appropriate intensity of emotions?

2. "Great effects upon the body certainly are no sure evidences that affections are spiritual." Scripture often emphasizes the weakness of the flesh, as unsuited for great spiritual tasks (Matthew 26:41; 1 Corinthians 15:9-10). Yet there are times when our bodies are profoundly moved by experiences of God's presence (Habbakuk 3:16; Psalm 119:120; Daniel 10:8; Revelation 1:17). How then do we distinguish mere emotionalism from those demonstrations of emotion with spiritual consequences?

3. Neither fluency of talk, fervency of expression, nor a flood of communication are a true sign of God's Spirit within us. Yet it is also true that "out of the abundance of the heart, the mouth speaks." The issue, then, is how long does the effect last? (See Proverbs 25:14; 2 Peter 2:17; Jude 4, 11.)

4. True affections for God cannot be stimulated falsely, "worked up psychologically," or otherwise manipulated. Examine the circumstances, the stimuli, and the motives for

such forms of emotional manipulation in your own experiences. Do you ever see God's *Holy* Spirit playing such deceitful tricks on us? Discuss Hebrews 6:4-5,9.

Further Forms of Misguidedness (pp. 44-69)

1. The use of Scripture may be abused, as in a sudden thought or text, for cannot Satan also quote Scripture as he did when he tempted Jesus in the wilderness? Do we not experience how neurotically some people can misinterpret a text to fit in with their own neurosis? Cite other ways a text can be used inappropriately.

2. Cannot even our loving affections be misdirected, or the sudden impulse to say something positive be forgotten about later? Is it appropriate for a pastor in a church service to ask you to turn around during the service and say, "I love you" to your neighbor? (Discuss Ephesians 6:24.)

3. Counterfeits abound all around us. Read about Naaman, 2 Kings 5:10-14, 17-18; Balaam and Balak, Numbers 23; the parable of the Sower, Matthew 13:110; the professing believers who fall away, Matthew 24:12-13. Jesus speaks of those who for a time enjoyed the light of John the Baptist (John 5:35).

4. Consolations and comforts in themselves may not be evidences of true Christian life, while real Christians may have to go through "the dark night of the soul" in desolations and distresses. Examine the fickle emotional life of Saul in his relations with David (1 Samuel 17-31). In Scripture, observes Edwards, "nowhere is described the Spirit's method of producing the fruit of the Spirit." Instead, they are described (Galatians 5:22-23). As His ways are inscrutable (John 3:8), we cannot judge superficially by emotional cause-and-effect sequences. How have we seen this in the stories of conversions we have heard? What other signs does Edwards discount as being valid, such as time and effort invested, verbal worship, self-confidence, outward signs, etc.?

PART THREE
HOW TRULY GRACIOUS AFFECTIONS FOR GOD ARE KNOWN

It is the aesthetic delight of the loveliness of God that draws out the true affections of the Christian, argues Edwards. The leading of the Spirit "consists in a person's being guarded by a spiritual and distinguishing taste of that which has in it true moral beauty." This knowledge then is intuitive rather than discursive, yet it "sanctifies the reason, and causes it to be open and free," as well as positively helping reason to be clearer and more strongly convinced. Spirit longings are also deepened, for "the more a true saint loves with a gracious love, the more he desires to love God." Likewise, "the more he hates sin, the more he desires to hate it." Indeed, a great love requires also a great hate of all that would distort or destroy what is good.

What Is True Spirituality? (pp. 73-87)

1. Edwards prefaces this section with personal humility, that we are never sure or clear enough that we can ever confidently say, "I know what true spirituality is." Likewise, we should be careful not to be overconfident that we know all about it. What distinguishes true dogma from dogmaticism?
2. Can "worldly" or "stuck" Christians be expected to discern wisely?
3. Are "rules" adequate to define what we mean by "spiritual" or authentic emotions and affections in the Christian life?
4. Only the Holy Spirit makes us to be truly "spiritual" (1 Corinthians 2:13-14). So "gracious affections" are the gift of His Spirit to us. Discuss the implications of such insight in the context of our contemporary confusion about "spirituality," both secular and religious. How important then is Edwards' teaching today? (See pp. 76-87.)

The Beauty and Glory of God in Jesus Christ Is the Basis of Gracious Affections (pp. 89-97)

1. The projective nature of true affections for God implies that we do not have them in ourselves, but in God and Jesus

Christ. How far then should we be preoccupied with our own emotions?

2. Primarily we are to love God for His own sake, not only for what he has done or what we anticipate He may do for us. Does this reorientate your attitudes toward God, and your motives for gratitude toward God?

3. "Spiritual" in the New Testament has nothing to do with the human spirit or "soul," for this too is "carnal" or "of the flesh." Rather it relates solely to the work and presence of the Holy Spirit (see question 4 above). If it reflects only the indwelling of the Holy Spirit in the life of Christians, how does it help us redefine the place of our emotions and affections in Christian experience?

4. How then does the Christian differ from the nonChristian in the interpretation and evaluation of his or her own emotions and affections?

It Is Moral Excellence That Enlightens the Spiritually Minded (pp. 97-116)

1. Discuss what Edwards means by "moral," "divine excellence," and "holiness."

2. The Scriptures represent the saints adoring the loveliness of God's holiness. Do we still do this? If not, why has this been dimmed or even lost among contemporary Christians?

3. How is spiritual understanding to be received and nurtured?

4. Likewise, how are we to understand the Scriptures spiritually? Is even proper exegesis enough?

Certainty and Humility in Gracious Affections (pp. 117-139)

1. What of the reality of Christ have you experienced personally? How has this strengthened and stabilized your faith as a Christian?

2. What is "spiritual conviction?" How does it guard us from *deception*?

3. What is meant by "evangelical humiliation"?

4. What are the traits of Christian humility in daily experience?

Gracious Affections Transform Our Character (pp. 141-165)

1. Is conversion "once-for-all" or is it also a continuous process of change within our lives?
2. Edwards was much indebted to a previous New England Puritan teacher—Thomas Shepard, especially to his book *The Ten Virgins*. How does this parable (Matthew 25:1-14) teach us, as it did these writers, about the ongoing life of the Christian? Do we not need continuously to discern the difference between "my spirit" and "the Holy Spirit" if we seek to be indwelt by Him?
3. What qualities of Christlikeness does Edwards focus upon?
4. Why are tenderness, gentleness, and a childlike spirit so often emphasized by God's saints, as Edwards too emphasizes them?

Balance and Practice of Gracious Affections (pp. 157-188)

1. "There is symmetry and beauty in God's workmanship." Discuss what Edwards appreciates about such "spiritual balance" in the Christian life.
2. How is such "balance" related to the consistency of true Christian character? Traditionally moral theologians have emphasized the cultivation of "the virtuous life," yet this is wholly absent in Edwards' teaching. Is there a doctrinal reason for this?
3. Actually, in the full text of Edwards' treatise, the closing section or "twelfth sign of gracious affections" is half as long as all the other "eleven signs." Why should the *practice* of these affections be so vital?
4. "Nothing can be more practical than divine grace in the heart." Is this really true in our Christian experience? Elaborate upon the meaning of this for contemporary Christianity.

Many more issues might be explored from the challenge of Edwards' treatise. But enumerate ways in which this book could be used to deal with so much contemporary confusion about "WHO IS A CHRISTIAN?"